First World War
and Army of Occupation
War Diary
France, Belgium and Germany

21 DIVISION
Divisional Troops
Royal Army Veterinary Corps
33 Mobile Veterinary Section
1 September 1915 - 31 March 1919

WO95/2148/4

The Naval & Military Press Ltd
www.nmarchive.com
Published in association with The National Archives

Published by

The Naval & Military Press Ltd

Unit 10 Ridgewood Industrial Park,

Uckfield, East Sussex,

TN22 5QE England

Tel: +44 (0) 1825 749494

www.naval-military-press.com

www.nmarchive.com

This diary has been reprinted in facsimile from the original. Any imperfections are inevitably reproduced and the quality may fall short of modern type and cartographic standards.

Contents

Document type	Place/Title	Date From	Date To
Heading	WO95/2148/4 33 Mobile Vetinary Service		
Heading	21st Division 33rd Mobile Vety Secn Sep 1915-Mar 1919		
War Diary	Field	01/09/1915	30/09/1915
Heading	21st Division 33rd Mob. Vet. Sect. Vol 2 Oct. 15		
War Diary	Liettres	01/10/1915	01/10/1915
War Diary	Morbeque	02/10/1915	02/10/1915
War Diary	Hondeghem	03/10/1915	08/10/1915
War Diary	Merris	09/10/1915	31/10/1915
Heading	21st Division 33rd Mob. Vet. Sect. Vol. 3 Nov. 15		
War Diary	Merris	01/11/1915	11/11/1915
War Diary	Nieppe	12/11/1915	30/11/1915
Heading	21st Division 33rd Mob. Vet. Sect. Vol 4		
War Diary	Nieppe	01/12/1915	31/12/1915
Heading	21st 33rd Mob. Vet. Sect. Vol 5 Jan 1916		
War Diary	Nieppe	01/01/1916	31/01/1916
Heading	33 M. V. S. 21st Div. Vol 6		
War Diary	Nieppe	01/02/1916	29/02/1916
Heading	33 M Vet S Vol 7		
War Diary	Nieppe	01/03/1916	22/03/1916
War Diary	Caestre	23/03/1916	02/04/1916
War Diary	Ribemont	02/04/1916	14/05/1916
War Diary	Abbeville	14/05/1916	15/05/1916
War Diary	Ribemont	16/05/1916	30/06/1916
Miscellaneous	D.A.A. & Q.M.G. 21st Division	31/07/1916	31/07/1916
War Diary	Ribemont	01/07/1916	04/07/1916
War Diary	Ally-Sur-Somme	05/07/1916	12/07/1916
War Diary	Ribemont	13/07/1916	20/07/1916
War Diary	Cavillon	21/07/1916	23/07/1916
War Diary	Le Cauroy	24/07/1916	31/07/1916
War Diary	Habarcq	01/08/1916	16/08/1916
War Diary	Agnes-Les-Duisans	16/08/1916	31/08/1916
War Diary	Le Cauroy	10/09/1916	13/09/1916
War Diary	Buire	13/09/1916	17/09/1916
War Diary	Fricourt	17/09/1916	21/09/1916
War Diary	Agnez-Les-Duisans	01/09/1916	05/09/1916
War Diary	Le-Cauroy	05/09/1916	09/09/1916
War Diary	Fricourt	22/09/1916	02/10/1916
War Diary	Ribemont	02/10/1916	03/10/1916
War Diary	St. Sauveur	03/10/1916	04/10/1916
War Diary	Famechon	04/10/1916	08/10/1916
War Diary	Noeux-Les-Mines	09/10/1916	04/01/1917
War Diary	Bethune	05/01/1917	27/01/1917
War Diary	Hazebrouck	28/01/1917	28/01/1917
War Diary	Herzeele	29/01/1917	12/02/1917
War Diary	Hazebroucke	13/02/1917	13/02/1917
War Diary	Bethune	14/02/1917	15/02/1917
War Diary	Noeux-Les-Mines	16/02/1917	03/03/1917
War Diary	Bethune	04/03/1917	10/03/1917
War Diary	Heuchin	11/03/1917	12/03/1917

War Diary	Aubrometz	13/03/1917	13/03/1917
War Diary	Bonnieres	14/03/1917	14/03/1917
War Diary	Doullens	15/03/1917	31/03/1917
War Diary	Gouy-En-Artois	01/04/1917	02/04/1917
War Diary	Bailleulmont	03/04/1917	04/04/1917
War Diary	Adinfer	05/04/1917	26/04/1917
War Diary	Boisleux-Au-Mont	27/04/1917	12/05/1917
War Diary	Adinfer	13/05/1917	31/05/1917
War Diary	Boisleux	01/06/1917	20/06/1917
War Diary	Adinfer	21/06/1917	01/07/1917
War Diary	Boisleux-Au-Mont	02/07/1917	01/08/1917
War Diary	Boiry St Rictrude	02/08/1917	26/08/1917
War Diary	Agnez-Les-Duisans	27/08/1917	16/09/1917
War Diary	Caestre	17/09/1917	24/09/1917
War Diary	Meteren	25/09/1917	29/09/1917
War Diary	La Clytte	30/09/1917	01/10/1917
War Diary	Zevecoten	02/10/1917	09/10/1917
War Diary	Racquingham	10/10/1917	20/10/1917
War Diary	Reninghelst	21/10/1917	21/10/1917
War Diary	La Clyte	22/10/1917	16/11/1917
War Diary	Doulieu	17/11/1917	18/11/1917
War Diary	Bellerive	19/11/1917	19/11/1917
War Diary	Hersin	20/11/1917	22/11/1917
War Diary	Anzin	23/11/1917	01/12/1917
War Diary	Beaulencourt	02/12/1917	02/12/1917
War Diary	Boucly	03/12/1917	03/12/1917
War Diary	Tincourt	04/12/1917	04/12/1917
War Diary	Villers Faucon	05/12/1917	12/01/1918
War Diary	Quinconce	13/01/1918	28/02/1918
War Diary	Le Quinconce	01/03/1918	02/03/1918
War Diary	Peronne	03/03/1918	10/03/1918
War Diary	Driencourt	11/03/1918	21/03/1918
War Diary	Driencourt & Fevillaucourt	22/03/1918	22/03/1918
War Diary	Clery-Hem Bray-Sur-Somme	23/03/1918	25/03/1918
War Diary	Etinehem Vaux Sur Somme	25/03/1918	26/03/1918
War Diary	Baizieux Contay	26/03/1918	26/03/1918
War Diary	Contay	27/03/1918	27/03/1918
War Diary	Bavelincourt	28/03/1918	30/03/1918
War Diary	Cardonnette	31/03/1918	31/03/1918
War Diary	Cardonnette Hangest	01/04/1918	01/04/1918
War Diary	Pesel Hoek Locre	02/04/1918	04/04/1918
War Diary	Dranoutre	04/04/1918	11/04/1918
War Diary	Heksken	11/04/1918	15/04/1918
War Diary	Heksken Wippenhoek	16/04/1918	30/04/1918
War Diary	St Jan-Ter-Biezen	30/04/1918	30/04/1918
War Diary	Near St Jan-Ter-Biezen	01/05/1918	01/05/1918
War Diary	Lederzeele	02/05/1918	03/05/1918
War Diary	Arques	04/05/1918	05/05/1918
War Diary	In Train Ferme de St Antoine near La Gery	06/05/1918	14/05/1918
War Diary	Vadiville Near Farm	14/05/1918	14/05/1918
War Diary	Vaux Varennes	15/05/1918	17/05/1918
War Diary	Vadiville Farm	18/05/1918	25/05/1918
War Diary	Bois De Cuissat	26/05/1918	27/05/1918
War Diary	Rosnay	28/05/1918	28/05/1918
War Diary	Ville en Tardenois	29/05/1918	29/05/1918
War Diary	La Neuville	30/05/1918	31/05/1918

War Diary	Soulieres	01/06/1918	03/06/1918
War Diary	Courjeonnet	04/06/1918	09/06/1918
War Diary	Verdey Moeurs	10/06/1918	14/06/1918
War Diary	Fere-Champenoise	13/06/1918	14/06/1918
War Diary	Pont De Remy	15/06/1918	15/06/1918
War Diary	Cerisy-Buleux	16/06/1918	21/06/1918
War Diary	Baromesnil	22/06/1918	29/06/1918
War Diary	Oisemont	30/06/1918	01/07/1918
War Diary	Bourdon	02/07/1918	02/07/1918
War Diary	Canaples	03/07/1918	03/07/1918
War Diary	Raincheval	04/07/1918	24/08/1918
War Diary	Mailly Maillet	25/08/1918	30/08/1918
War Diary	Grandcourt	31/08/1918	05/09/1918
War Diary	Le Sars	06/09/1918	06/09/1918
War Diary	Beaulencourt	07/09/1918	15/09/1918
War Diary	Le Mesnil	16/09/1918	29/09/1918
War Diary	Equancourt	30/09/1918	30/09/1918
Heading	War Diary 33rd Mobile Veterinary Section October 1st-31st 1918		
War Diary	Equancourt	01/10/1918	06/10/1918
War Diary	Gouzeaucourt	07/10/1918	10/10/1918
War Diary	Bantouzelle	10/10/1918	10/10/1918
War Diary	Walincourt	11/10/1918	21/10/1918
War Diary	Montigny	22/10/1918	23/10/1918
War Diary	Inchy	24/10/1918	29/10/1918
War Diary	Neuvilly	30/10/1918	31/10/1918
Heading	War Diary Of 33rd Mobile Veterinary Section From 1st November 1918 To 30th November 1918 Vol 40		
War Diary	Neuvilly	01/11/1918	05/11/1918
War Diary	Poix Du Nord	05/11/1918	05/11/1918
War Diary	Locquignol	06/11/1918	09/11/1918
War Diary	La Grand Carriere	09/11/1918	30/11/1918
Heading	War Diary Of 33rd Mobile Veterinary Section R.A.V.C. From December 1st To December 31st 1918		
War Diary	La Grande Carriere	01/12/1918	17/12/1918
War Diary	Ovilliers	18/12/1918	18/12/1918
War Diary	Inchy Beaumont	19/12/1918	19/12/1918
War Diary	Aubencheul	20/12/1918	20/12/1918
War Diary	Buire	21/12/1918	21/12/1918
War Diary	Proyart	22/12/1918	22/12/1918
War Diary	Glisy	23/12/1918	23/12/1918
War Diary	Ailly-Sur-Somme	24/12/1918	29/12/1918
War Diary	Dreuil	30/12/1918	31/12/1918
Miscellaneous	Copy Of Letter From Major S.J. Chittenden To General Sir Hubert Gough		
Heading	War Diary Of 33rd Mobile Veterinary Section, R.A.V.C. From 1st January 1919 To 31st January 1919 Vol 42		
War Diary	Dreuil	01/01/1919	31/01/1919
Heading	21 Div War Diary Of 33rd Mobile Veterinary, R.A.V.C. From 1st February 1919 To 28th February 1919 Vol 33		
War Diary	Dreuil-Les-Amiens	01/02/1919	22/02/1919
War Diary	Hornoy	01/03/1919	17/03/1919
War Diary	Picquigny	18/03/1919	31/03/1919

W095

2148/4

33 Mobile Vetting Services

21ST DIVISION

33RD MOBILE VETY SECN

SEP 1915 - MAR 1919

Instructions regarding War Diaries and Intelligence Summaries are contained in F. S. Regs., Part II. and the Staff Manual respectively. Title pages will be prepared in manuscript.

WAR DIARY
or
INTELLIGENCE SUMMARY.
(Erase heading not required.)

Army Form C. 2118.

33rd Mobile Vety. Section
92

OFFICER-IN-[illegible]
No. 28 MAY 1919
ROYAL ARMY VETY. CORPS.

Place	Date	Hour	Summary of Events and Information	Remarks and references to Appendices
Field	6.9.15	9 a.m.	Riding school for 5 men who are not up to average standard.	
		11 a.m.	Evacuated 18 horses 2 mules to Bordon Hospital	
			a/Sergt. WILSON was kicked by a horse & was taken to Hospital	
		2 p.m.	Rifle Inspection. Ranging Practice for half of section	
		3 p.m.	Ranging Practice for remaining half of section	
"	7.9.15	10 p.m.	A.D.V.S. inspected section	
			Received large quantity of ordnance stores from ALDERSHOT	
			a/Sergt. WILSON returned to duty from Hospital	
	8.9.15	9 a.m.	Riding school for backward men	
		2 p.m.	Rifle Inspection. Lecture on sighting of rifle 3 p.m. final kit inspection	
		3 p.m.	Commenced arranging loading of waggons.	
			Two G.S. waggons attached to us for move overseas reported	
	9.9.15	9 a.m.	Finished loading scheme for waggons	
	10.9.15	12 a.m.	Completed loading of section 2 limbered waggons	
			Received orders from A.D.V.S. for move overseas on the 11[illegible] ...ement at different stages from Div. Hd. Qrs.	

1577 Wt. W10791/1773 500,000 1/15 D. D. & L. A.D.S.S./Forms/C. 2118.

Instructions regarding War Diaries and Intelligence Summaries are contained in F. S. Regs., Part II. and the Staff Manual respectively. Title pages will be prepared in manuscript.

WAR DIARY
or
INTELLIGENCE SUMMARY. 33rd Mobile Vety Section 94
(Erase heading not required.)

Army Form C. 2118.

Place	Date	Hour	Summary of Events and Information	Remarks and references to Appendices
Field	13.9.15	11.15 AM	Arrived AUDRICQ. Was met by another interpreter M[illegible] with an order fr Div. Hd. Qrs. for him to report to me, in place of M. DUCROIS. Ordered latter to report Div. Hd. Qrs.	
		12 AM	Received orders to proceed to WATTEN. The sanitary section were placed under my charge to proceed to same place	
		1.45 pm	Arrived WATTEN & found Div. Hd. Qrs. there. Met A.D.V.S. (Major Macdonald) & proceeded to billets with one squadron of South Irish Horse.	
	14.9.15	11 AM	Commenced re arranging of transport. All animals [illegible] travelled well except one riding with a severely contused [illegible] with Laminitis Acute. The latter will probably not be a[illegible]	
	15.9.15	9 A.M.	Proceeded ST. OMER with D.A.D.O[illegible]	
	16.9.15	—	Nothing of note	
	17.9.15	10 AM	All available officers of Division ~~reported~~ [illegible] reference to meet the General of [illegible] Received various orders fr Hd Qrs Div[illegible]	
	18.9.15	8 A.M.	Sergt. Peapell, my senior N.C.O. repo[illegible]	

Instructions regarding War Diaries and Intelligence Summaries are contained in F. S. Regs., Part II. and the Staff Manual respectively. Title pages will be prepared in manuscript. Continued

Army Form C. 2118.

WAR DIARY
or
INTELLIGENCE SUMMARY. 33rd Mobile Vety. Section 96

(Erase heading not required.)

Place	Date	Hour	Summary of Events and Information	Remarks and references to Appendices
Field	21.9.15	5pm	Received orders to move at 5.25 p.m.	
"	22.9.15	2 am	arrived AIRE. proceeded to field on AIRE-LOMBRES road. at 3 pm	
"		10 am	Evacuated 10 horses 2 mules for AIRE Station	
"	23.9.15	4 pm	Received orders to move at 8 pm. My position to be immediately the D.A.C. Proceeded to LIETRES arriving at 11.45 p.m.	
"	24.9.15	10	Reported position of section to ADVS at FERFAY	
	25.9.15	2 pm	The billet was very bad & decided to move. Completed move at 4 p.m.	
"		8 pm	Received orders to march at 10 p.m. behind DAC Marched all night by way of MARLES-LES-MINES. All horses that had been sent to section were able to travel. Camped in a field	
	26.9.15	5 am	near HOUCHIN. Rested until 2 p.m when orders came to proceed to NOEUX-LES-MINES arrived 7 p.m.	
		8 p.m.	Evacuated 16 horses	
			The orders for moving received from Div. Hd Qrs have been very vague. On three occasions ... & be at an appointed place three miles away ...	

Instructions regarding War Diaries and Intelligence Summaries are contained in F. S. Regs., Part II. and the Staff Manual respectively. Title pages will be prepared in manuscript.

WAR DIARY
or
INTELLIGENCE SUMMARY.
(Erase heading not required.)

Army Form C. 2118.

33rd Mobile Vety Section

97

Place	Date	Hour	Summary of Events and Information	Remarks and references to Appendices
Field	27.9.18	10 AM	Reported position to A D V S who was at MAZINGARGE with Div. Hd Qrs. The food supply of section failed on account of supply wagon of Div. Train getting lost in neighbourhood of trenches. This was the first time that our rations had failed. A.D.V.S. gave orders for 1 corporal & 4 men to be placed on the main BETHUNE Road in front of MAZINGARGE, ~~the~~ to form an advanced collecting station. This camp was well placed near artillery lines. Men in position at 6 P.M.	
		8 pm.	Evacuated 16 animals to Base.	
	28.9.18	8 a.m	Visited advanced collecting post & arranged fresh accomodation for the men	
		2 pm.	Received a consignment medicines which were greatly needed	
			The riders & transport horses ~~of~~ section have stood ~~the~~ strain of the last six days very well. Some of the men however are greatly in need of a rest.	
	29.9.18	11 a.m	Visited adv. collecting station & destroyed two animals of 9 Div. ...	
		2 pm	A.D.V.S. inspected section	
		4 pm	Collected a batch of 7 horses for D.A.C. 9 Div ...	
	30.9.18		Nothing of note. One man Orange... post sick & admitted to 63rd Field Amb...	

1577 Wt. W10791/1773 500,000 1/15 D. D. & L. A.D.S.S./Forms/C. 2118.

Instructions regarding War Diaries and Intelligence Summaries are contained in F. S. Regs., Part II. and the Staff Manual respectively. Title pages will be prepared in manuscript. [illegible] 18.9.15

Army Form C. 2118.

WAR DIARY
or
INTELLIGENCE SUMMARY.
(Erase heading not required.)

33rd Mobile Vety Section
95

Place	Date	Hour	Summary of Events and Information	Remarks and references to Appendices
Field	–	–	to [illegible] field. Sentenced him to 14 Days F.P. No. [illegible]	
"	19.9.15	8 pm	Received orders to move 2 hours notice	
"	20.9.15	10 A.M.	Received orders to move at 8 p.m. A.D.V.S. issued orders that a small collecting station had to be established on main ST. OMER road, men to be in position by 7 30 p.m. Sent 4 men & 1 corporal. The whole of horses of division passed this point between 8 p.m. & 11 p.m. As the position of the collecting post had been notified by a special order, this greatly facilitated the collection of sick animals. 18 animals were collected.	
		10.15 pm	Remainder of section joined collecting station & all moved off at 11 p.m for ARQUES. In passing through ST. OMER Pte HAYGREEN was injured (broken leg) through horse rolling on him. Taken to R.T.O. & later collected by Stationary Hospital. ~~Evacuated~~	
"	21.9.15	8 A.M.	Evacuated 18 horses to Base.	
		2.30	Arrived ARQUES. No billets so encamped in side road.	
		10 A.M.	Reported in person my position to ADVS at Div. Hd. Qrs. RACKENHEM	
		2 pm	Evacuated 3 horses	

Instructions regarding War Diaries and Intelligence Summaries are contained in F. S. Regs., Part II. and the Staff Manual respectively. Title pages will be prepared in manuscript. Continued

WAR DIARY
or
INTELLIGENCE SUMMARY. 33rd Mobile Vety. Section 96

(Erase heading not required.)

Army Form C. 2118.

Place	Date	Hour	Summary of Events and Information	Remarks and references to Appendices
Contd	21.9.15	5 pm	Received orders to move at 5.25 p.m.	
	22.9.15	2 am	arrived AIRE – proceeded to field on AIRE–LOMBRES road at 3 am	
		10 am	Evacuated 10 horses 2 mules from AIRE Station	
	23.9.15	4 pm	Received orders to move at 8 pm. My position to be immediately [behind] the DAC. Proceeded to LIETRES arriving at 11.45 pm	
	24.9.15	10 am	Reported position of section to ADVS at FERFAY	
	25.9.15	2 pm	The billet was very bad & decided to move. Completed move at 4 pm	
		8 pm	Received orders to march at 10 pm behind DAC. Marched all night by way of MARLES-LES-MINES. All horses that had been sent to section were able to march. Camped in a field	
	26.9.15	5 am	near HOUCHIN. Rested until 2 pm when orders came to proceed to NOEUX-LES-MINES arrived 4 pm	
		8 pm	Evacuated 16 horses	
			The orders for moving received from the DAC & us during the last few days have been very vague. On three occasions I have received orders to move & be at an adjoining place three miles away in 20 minutes	

Instructions regarding War Diaries and Intelligence Summaries are contained in F. S. Regs., Part II. and the Staff Manual respectively. Title pages will be prepared in manuscript.

WAR DIARY or INTELLIGENCE SUMMARY.

(Erase heading not required.)

Army Form C. 2118.

33rd Mobile Vety Section

97

29 MAY 1919

Place	Date	Hour	Summary of Events and Information	Remarks and references to Appendices
Field	27.9.18	10 AM	Reported position to ADVS who was at MAZINGARGE with Div. Hd Qrs. The food supply of section failed on account of supply waggon of Div. Train getting lost in neighbourhood of trenches. This was the first time that our rations had failed. ADVS gave orders for 1 corporal & 4 men to be placed on the main BETHUNE road in front of MAZINGARGE, to form an advanced collecting station. This camp was well placed near artillery lines. Men in position at 6 p.m.	
		8 p.m.	Evacuated 16 animals to Base.	
	28.9.18	8 a.m.	Visited advanced collecting post & arranged brush accomodation for the men.	
		2 p.m.	Received a consignment medicines which were greatly needed. The riders & transport lines of section have stood the strain of the last six days very well. Some of the men however are greatly in need of a rest.	
	29.9.18	11 a.m.	Visited adv. collecting station & destroyed two animals of 9th Div. with shell wounds.	
		2 p.m.	ADVS inspected section	
		4 p.m.	Collected a batch of 7 horses from DAC 9th Div. & evac. to Base.	
	30.9.18		Nothing of note. One man brought back from adv. collecting post sick & admitted to 63rd Field Ambulance	

J. Hogg Capt. a
V.O. i/c G.H.Q.

1577 Wt. W10791/1773 300,000 1/15 D. D. & L. A.D.S.S./Forms/C. 2118.

21st Division

121/7608

33rd Mob: Vet: Sect

Vol 2

Oct 15

Instructions regarding War Diaries and Intelligence Summaries are contained in F. S. Regs., Part II. and the Staff Manual respectively. Title pages will be prepared in manuscript.

Sept 1915

WAR DIARY
or
INTELLIGENCE SUMMARY. 33rd MOBILE VETY SECTION

(Erase heading not required.)

Army Form C. 2118.

91

28 MAY 1919

Place	Date	Hour	Summary of Events and Information	Remarks and references to Appendices
Field 1-9-15	1-9-15	7.45 AM	Visited 94 Bde R.F.A. to see horse with suspected skin disease. Placed under isolation	
		10 AM	Evacuated 16 horses from Vety Hospital WITLEY CAMP to Vety Hospital BORDON.	
		12 AM	Pte CANT charged with insolence to N.C.O. Charge dismissed	
		2 pm	Rifle inspection	
"	2-9-15	9 a.m.	Riding school. Every man in Section passed out	
		12 AM	Col. SAWYER visited lines & remarked on good condition of horses, though several were rather small. Cooking arrangements good	
	3-9-15	9 AM	Received orders from Div. Hd. Qrs. that all numbers & names of units had to be painted out. The special sign 11 to be painted on tailboard of each vehicle.	
		10 AM	Set out for ALDERSHOT to visit Ordnance stores. Great difficulty in procuring clothing.	
		11 pm	Visited lines - found all correct.	
	4-9-15		Nothing of note	
	5-9-15	10 AM	L.D. horse admitted at 8 AM. died from Volvulus. Formed an agreement with Mr RICHARDS PEASMARCH near Godalming to collect carcases of all animals	
		11 AM	Kit inspection. All correct except many men needing new jackets & breeches	
		3 pm	All men received 1st innoc (enteric) by M.O. 94 Bde R.F.A.	

33 Mobile Vet Section

Instructions regarding War Diaries and Intelligence Summaries are contained in F. S. Regs., Part II. and the Staff Manual respectively. Title Pages will be prepared in manuscript.

WAR DIARY
or
~~INTELLIGENCE SUMMARY~~
(Erase heading not required.)

Army Form C. 2118

Place	Date	Hour	Summary of Events and Information	Remarks and references to Appendices
LIETTRE ~~MORBEQUE~~	1.10.15		Left at 10.30 a.m. to join Div Train on Aire Road about 3 Kilometres from town. Before leaving discharged one HD horse fracture of humerus. Quarrelled with Maire of village re burial. Evacuated 8 horses at Aire in passing through. Reached Morbeque at 5.15 p.m. Billets good	
Morbeque	2.10.15	10.15 am	Left Morbeque. Passed through Hazebrouck to Pradelle at 2.15 pm. Waited on road with other troops to get definite orders re billeting area. Orders came 5 pm to proceed to Hondeghem. Reached this place 6.15 pm. Occupied Farm house with field adjoining. Water supply poor.	
Hondeghem	3.10.15	9.15 am	Visited Field Remount ~~Section~~ 2nd Army to examine chargers for Hd Qr Staff. Rode several & decided on one	
"	4.10.15	9 a.m.	Received one charger for treatment – Helminthiasis. DDOS inspected section – expressed satisfaction. Suggested indenting for lighter picketing ropes with 3 strands wire running through	
"	5.10.15		Evacuated 16 horses to Neufchatel. Received orders at 12.15 to proceed to Mervis on following day	
"	6.10.15		Evacuated 8 horses. Visited Field Remount Section & 64 Field Ambulance. Moved out of billets at 11.45 a.m. arriving at Mervis 2 pm. Good billets. D.D.V.S. 2 Army visited section. At 11.45 pm proceeded to Hd Qrs to attend sick horse	
"	7.10.15	9 am	Visited farms near Pradelle to inspect cattle suspected of Foot & Mouth Disease. Four cases in Milch cows at M Paul Leroy in village. Farm closed to troops. Evacuated 8 animals to Neufchatel	
"	8.10.15	7.15 am	Rode to M. Paul London to collect one H.D. horse belonging 46 D.A.C. also one charger	

1875 Wt. W593/826 1,000,000 4/15 J.B.C. & A. A.D.S.S./Forms/C. 2118.

2/

33 Mobile Vety Secn

Army Form C. 2118

Instructions regarding War Diaries and Intelligence Summaries are contained in F. S. Regs., Part II. and the Staff Manual respectively. Title Pages will be prepared in manuscript.

WAR DIARY
or
~~INTELLIGENCE SUMMARY~~
(Erase heading not required.)

Place	Date	Hour	Summary of Events and Information	Remarks and references to Appendices
			at M. Emile Moquet Vieux-Berquin. This animal removed in float being too lame to walk	
Merris ~~9/10/15~~		4 pm 15	Visited HQ Qrs Staff charger 2 Army with influenza Hazebrouck	
	9 10 15	8 am	Visited Field Remount Section – collected one charger. Evacuated 24 animals from Caestre	
~~10/10/15~~	10 10 15	8 am	Visited 63 & 64 Field Ambulances at Pradelle & Caestre. Admitted three horses Div HQ Qrs for treatment.	
		1 pm	DDR inspected horses of section & expressed satisfaction	
		4 pm	Visited HQ Qr Sig Co horses	
~~11/10/15~~	11/10/15	8.30 am	Evacuated 8 horses Neuf Chelle	
12/10	12/10/15	9 am	Went to office DDOS 2 Army to report ~~Boned~~ Evacuated 8 animals	
		2 pm	Attended inspection infantry transport by General Forestier Walker. Paid men 770 frs	
"	13/10/15	9 am	Overhauled transport waggons	
		1 pm	Visited 63 Inf Bde ~~to~~ inspect mules	
"	14/10/15	9 am	Evacuated 8 animals General Forestier Walker inspected section section & expressed satisfaction	
		4 pm	Visited 64 Field Ambulance Admitted 2 horses for treatment	
"	15/10/15	8 am	Attended horse at Hazebrouck injured whilst detraining	
		11 am	Visited 63 Inf Brigade	
"	16/10/15	9 am	Went to Armentières with A.DOS to inspect horses of 94 Bde R.F.O. A few cases of mangy ~~Horses~~ looking well. Mules skin. Sent 1 Corpl. 2 men to GRAVES to collect	

Instructions regarding War Diaries and Intelligence Summaries are contained in F. S. Regs., Part II. and the Staff Manual respectively. Title Pages will be prepared in manuscript.

WAR DIARY or ~~INTELLIGENCE SUMMARY~~

33 Mobile Vety Section

(Erase heading not required.)

Army Form C. 2118

Place	Date	Hour	Summary of Events and Information	Remarks and references to Appendices
			2 horses K.O.Y.L.I. One horse issued to 62 Inf Bde, one to 8 lines.	
Morris	17/10/15	8 am	Visited lines Hazebrouck	
		9 am	Evacuated 8 animals Caestre.	
		2 pm	Sgt. [illegible] jaundice sent to No. 12 hospital [illegible]	
"	18/10/15	9 am	Visited lines Hazebrouck also 64 Field Amb.	
"	19/10/15	8.30 am	Visited [illegible] re Foot-mouth Disease. Several farms affected. All closed to Troops.	
		4 pm	Visited Nieppe to collect injured horse.	
"	20/10/15	9 am	Visited Bailleul admitted three horses for treatment	
"	21/10/15	10 am	Evacuated 8 animals to Caestre. Visited 64 Field Ambulance	
"	22/10/15	9 am	Visited Pradelle, Borre, Strazeele re Foot & Mouth in milch cows. Four farms affected. All closed to troops	
		1 pm	Evacuated 6 horses to Caestre.	
"	23/10/15	8 am	Hazebrouck to dress wounded horse. Visited 64 Field Ambulance	
"	24/10/15	8 am	Hazebrouck to dress horse. #	
		12 am	Held a[n] exhibition of best turn out of man horse & saddlery. Great success	
		2 pm.	Visited Nieppe to examine 2 cases 96 Bde R.F.A. Both ringworm	
"	25/10/15	9.30 am	Received Hd. Qr. charge suspected [illegible] scabies. Visited 64 Field Ambulance. Ordered three horses for evacuation	
"	26/10/15	9 am	Evacuated 12 animals. Brought injured horse from Hazebrouck in float. Visited 62 Inf Brigade	

1875 Wt. W593/826 1,000,000 4/15 J.B.C. & A. A.D.S.S./Forms/C. 2118.

Instructions regarding War Diaries and Intelligence Summaries are contained in F. S. Regs., Part II. and the Staff Manual respectively. Title Pages will be prepared in manuscript.

33 Mobile Vety Sect

WAR DIARY
or
~~INTELLIGENCE SUMMARY~~
(Erase heading not required.)

Army Form C. 2118

Place	Date	Hour	Summary of Events and Information	Remarks and references to Appendices
Merris	27/10/15	10 am	Discovered farm ? disease in farm in which billeted. Reported same to ADVS 21 Division. Cattle were seen in 2 cowsheds all showing ? lesions	
		2 pm	Received orders to move into another billet	
"	28/10/15	11 am	Moved section to another billet in village	
		1 pm	Motored to Cassel to inspect the charge of Sewell Gloves	
		3 pm	Received telegram to visit horses at Oxelaere belonging to Camp Commandant 2 Army	
"	29/10/15	10 am	Major Franklyn a DDS 50 Div visited section with OC Mob Vety Section of his Div. Quite satisfied with position. Agreed to take over billets when 50 Div moved into our area	
"	30/10/15	9 am	Visited 64 Field Ambulance. 10 horses ordered to section for evacuation. Sent in an order to CRE for materials to erect 2 standings for 30 horses each	
		3 pm	In afternoon received 12.000 bricks for standings	
"	31/10/15	9 am	Evacuated 8 horses. Went to Oxelaere to visit horse. Admitted 2 horses for treatment only	

J Hogg
for AVC
O.C 33 Mob Vety Section

1875 Wt. W593/826 1,000,000 4/15 J.B.C. & A. A.D.S.S./Forms/C. 2118.

21st Division

33rd Ind: Vet: Sect;
Vol: #3

121/7656

Nov 15

33rd Mobile Veterinary Section

Instructions regarding War Diaries and Intelligence Summaries are contained in F. S. Regs., Part II. and the Staff Manual respectively. Title Pages will be prepared in manuscript.

WAR DIARY
or
INTELLIGENCE SUMMARY
(Erase heading not required.)

Army Form C. 2118

Place	Date	Hour	Summary of Events and Information	Remarks and references to Appendices
MERRIS	1.11.15	9 am	Examined eleven Hd. Qr. Remounts for infections or contagious disease. All correct.	
		12am.	12 500 Bricks arrived from Armentieres for standings for animals. Very poor quality	
"	2.11.15	10 am	D.D.V.S. 2nd Army inspected section. Everything satisfactory	
		2 pm	Rifle inspection	
"	3.11.15	10 am.	Visited billet of 50 Division mobile section at NIEPPE which I arranged with O.C to take over. This is an excellent billet in every way.	
"	4.11.15	10 am	Went to STRAZEEL to try + hire horse float by the week. Not successful	
		10.30 am	Visited 64 Field Ambulance + ordered two horses into Mob. Vety. Sect.	
		1 pm.	Visited 63 Field Ambulance. Saw a case which was very suspicious of Glanders. ordered into mobile section for testing	
"	5.11.15	9 am	Commenced excavating for horse standing also made three large drains running through middle of field	
"		12 am	Parade of all Hd Qr. horses. Inspected by General	
		9 pm	Injected horse of 63 Field Ambulance with suspicious glanders	
"	6.11.15	10 am	Evacuated seven horses to NEUF CHATEL hospital. Microscope received from base	
		12 am	Received 3 500 bricks from HAZEBROUCK. Good quality. Rifle Inspection	[signature] O.C 33rd Mob Vety Sect

1875 Wt. W593/826 1,000,000 4/15 J.B.C. & A. A.D.S.S./Forms/C. 2118.

33rd Mobile Vety Section

Instructions regarding War Diaries and Intelligence Summaries are contained in F. S. Regs., Part II. and the Staff Manual respectively. Title Pages will be prepared in manuscript.

WAR DIARY
or
INTELLIGENCE SUMMARY
(Erase heading not required.)

Army Form C. 2118.

Place	Date	Hour	Summary of Events and Information	Remarks and references to Appendices
MERRIS	7.11.15	9 a.m	Admitted 7 horses for evacuation. One suspected Sarcoptic Mange. Scraping exam Negative	
"	8.11.15	10 a.m	Veterinary stores for base arrived. Received an enquiry from C.R.E. re his Charger.	
"	9.11.15	10 a.m	Made final arrangements re moving of section to NIEPPE.	
		2 p.m	D.D.V.S. visited Section	
"	10.11.15	9.15 a.m	Sent advance party to NIEPPE ~~two~~ 1 Corporal 3 men to make arrangements for section moving in	
		1 pm	Evacuated 8 animals from CAESTRE to NEUF CHATEL	
"	11.11.15	9 a.m.	Left MERRIS for NIEPPE arriving 1.15 p.m. Sent Corporal & one man for line of march to collect stray horses at STEENWERCK.	
NIEPPE	12.11.15	11 a.m	Went to STEENWERCK to see R.T.O. to see what notice he wanted for boxing animals. 24 hrs. notice required. Third floor to carry only lame cases to Station	
"	13/11/15	8.30 a.m	Evacuated 13 horses to NEUF-CHATEL. Examined five sample scrapings from 96 Bde R.F.A suspected mange. Negative	
"	14/11/15	11 a.m	A.D.V.S. inspected section. Section limbered waggons weighed at Mairie NIEPPE. Results telegraphed to D.D.V.S. 2 Army	
"	15/11/15	8.30 a.m	Evacuated 14 animals.	
		2 p.m	Visited 03 Field Ambulance	
	16/11/15	9 am	Received orders to erect a "Dug out" in my lines. Completed in six hours	

J Hogg Lt AVC
O.C. 33 Mob Vety Section

1875 Wt. W593/826 1,000,000 4/15 J.B.C. & A. A.D.S.S./Forms/C. 2118.

33rd Mobile Vety. Section

Instructions regarding War Diaries and Intelligence Summaries are contained in F. S. Regs., Part II. and the Staff Manual respectively. Title Pages will be prepared in manuscript.

WAR DIARY
or
INTELLIGENCE SUMMARY
(Erase heading not required.)

Army Form C. 2118.

Place	Date	Hour	Summary of Events and Information	Remarks and references to Appendices
NIEPPE	17/11/15	9 pm	Tested five horses for Glanders 95 Bde R.F.A. all Negative. Veterinary Stores arrived	
	18/11/15	9 am	Evacuated 16 horses from STEENWERCK.	
	19/11/15	10 am	Visited HQ. Qrs. re head collars for Remounts. Arrangements for collecting same unsatisfactory	
	20/11/15	10 am	A.D.V.S inspected equipment of Section. Everything satisfactory	
		2 pm	Visited Field Remount Section 2nd Army	
		9 pm	Injected 3 animals Mallein test. Negative	
	21/11/15	8.30 am	Evacuated 12 animals to NEUF CHATEL	
		3 pm	Pte J Millar sent to 63rd Field Ambulance suspected appendicitis	
			Local Corps order received ordering Sergt A Wilson to proceed to No 14 Vety Hospital	
	22/11/15	8 am	Visited 63 Field Ambulance inspected all animals	
		2 pm	Sergt. Wilson proceeded to STEENWERCK Station to report to R.T.O. prior to departing to No 14 Hospital	
	23/11/15	9 am	Sent out party of men to collect 3 Vet horses at Pont NIEPPE	
		12 am	Paid out 930 Francs to men of Section	
	24/11/15	10 am	Visited Baths at Pont Nieppe to arrange for men's weekly Bath. Decided on each Monday evening between 5 - 6 o'clock	
		2 pm	Examined 3 scrapings of O.C. 94 Bde R.F.A. suspected Mange. Negative	

Y Hogg [illegible] AVC
O.C 33 Mob Vety Secn

33 Mobile Vety Section

Instructions regarding War Diaries and Intelligence Summaries are contained in F. S. Regs., Part II. and the Staff Manual respectively. Title Pages will be prepared in manuscript.

WAR DIARY
or
INTELLIGENCE SUMMARY
(Erase heading not required.)

Army Form C. 2118.

Place	Date	Hour	Summary of Events and Information	Remarks and references to Appendices
NIEPPE	25/11/15	8.30 am	Evacuated 8 animals STEENWERCK to NEUF-CHATEL	
		11 am	Inspected Hd. Qrs Signal horses. Six cases Ringworm found	
		2.30 pm	Inspected 64 Field Ambulance horses Looking exceedingly well	
	26/11/15	8.30 am	Sent seven animals to STEENWERCK Station for evacuation but R.T.O. refused to box them as no telegram had been received concerning them	
		12 am	Enquired at 25 Div Hd Qrs re wire which was handed in previous day ordering a truck at Station. Found that mistake had occurred at this office the telegram now having been despatched	
	27/11/15	3.30 pm	D.D.V.S. 2nd Army arrived & gave demonstration to Officers (Vety) of division on Intra palpebral test for Glanders. Complained to A.D.V.S. of great difficulty of procuring head ropes from Ordnance	
	28/11/15	8.30 am	Evacuated 8 animals Received bale of Xmas for men of section from 'Daily Chronicle'	
		9 pm	Tested 3 horses by intra palpebral method for glanders	
	29/11/15	8.30 am	Evacuated 8 animals from STEENWERCK	
		4 pm	Men attended baths. This system of Divisional baths is extremely useful in small units	
	30/11/15	9 am	Visited Hd. Qrs. Chargers. Sent in report to A.D.V.S. on shoeing of same	J Hogg A.V.C. O.C. 33 Mob Vety Sec

21st Division

33rd Inf: Bde: Dec:
Vol: 4

121/7911

1.

33 Mobile Vety. Section

WAR DIARY
or
INTELLIGENCE SUMMARY
(Erase heading not required.)

Army Form C. 2118

Instructions regarding War Diaries and Intelligence Summaries are contained in F. S. Regs., Part II. and the Staff Manual respectively. Title Pages will be prepared in manuscript.

Place	Date	Hour	Summary of Events and Information	Remarks and references to Appendices
NIEPPE	1.12.15	9 a.m.	Vacated six sick animals to No. 13 Hospital Neuf Chatel.	
		12 am	Visited Hd. Qrs (Div) Armentieres to attend two horses suffering from shrapnel wounds.	
"	2.12.15	9 am	Received a supply of head ropes with thin strand of plaited wire running through. Sent as an experiment for "rope galls" [?]	
		10 am	Visited 64 Field Ambulance. Ordered two horses with necrotic wounds into Hospital	
		12 am	Visited Northumbd Pioneers at Armentieres to inspect charger horses. Many shells so did not stay long.	
		2 pm	D.D.V.S. 2nd Army visited section. Received notice that Div. General would visit section on following day	
"	3.12.15	9 am	Vacated 24 sick animals to Neuf Chatel.	
		12 am	Divisional General (Gen Jacob) visited section. Inspected horses (section) + horses on sick lines. Transport waggons + billets. Made various enquiries as to feeding of men + arrangements that I had made for weekly baths. Expressed satisfaction	
"	4.12.15	—	Nothing of note	
"	5.12.15	9 a.m.	Visited 63. 64 Field Ambulances.	
		12 pm	Visited two horses of 98 Coy R E with Mallein.	
"	6.12.15	9 a.m.	Horses tested showed nothing abnormal. Vacated 21 sick animals from Steenwerck [?] to Neuf Chatel.	

33. Mobile Vety. Section

Instructions regarding War Diaries and Intelligence Summaries are contained in F. S. Regs., Part II. and the Staff Manual respectively. Title Pages will be prepared in manuscript.

WAR DIARY
or
INTELLIGENCE SUMMARY
(Erase heading not required.)

Army Form C. 2118

Place	Date	Hour	Summary of Events and Information	Remarks and references to Appendices
NIEPPE	7.12.15	9 am	Vacated 8 sick animals from Steenwerck to NEUF-CHATEL. The majority of these cases are necrotic wounds & Debility.	
"	8.12.15	9 am	Vacated 15 animals to Neufchatel. Great difficulty in getting animals to station which are very lame as there are only two floats within reasonable distance. These are used by the local brewers for carriage of beer, & only on very rare occasions are they at liberty.	
	9.12.15	10 a.m	Many shells uncomfortably close to section.	
		2.30	2nd Army Commander (Gen. Plumer) visited section. Inspected section horses & sick lines. Also section transport.	
	10.12.15	9 am	Vacated 46 horses & 2 mules from Steenwerck to Neufchatel. 40 of these horses were debility (extreme) from 95th Ammn. Col. R.F.A. All horses ranged from 6 to 9 years old.	
	11.12.15	9 am	Vacated 8 sick animals to Neufchatel	
	12.12.15	10 am	Inspected 66 Remounts which arrived at Steenwerck for Division. The greater majority of these were L.D. Two cases ringworm & one strangles discovered.	
	13.12.15	2 pm	D.D.V.S. 2nd Army & A.D.V.S. called a meeting of V.O.'s of Division to arrange quickest method to carry out testing of animals of division. Mallein & syringes were kept in my charge.	

1875 Wt. W593/826 1,000,000 4/15 J.B.C. & A. A.D.S.S./Forms/C. 2118.

3.

33rd Mobile Vety. Section

WAR DIARY
or
INTELLIGENCE SUMMARY
(Erase heading not required.)

Army Form C. 2118

Instructions regarding War Diaries and Intelligence Summaries are contained in F. S. Regs., Part II. and the Staff Manual respectively. Title Pages will be prepared in manuscript.

Place	Date	Hour	Summary of Events and Information	Remarks and references to Appendices
NIEPPE	14.12.15	9 am	Vacated 8 animals from Steenwerck to Neuf Chatel	
		11 am	Tested by Intra Palpebral method for glanders 24 of section horses.	
		[illegible]	Issued a syringe & mallein to each V.O. of Division. Testing of horses commenced.	
		6 pm	All V.O's of Div. reported to A.D.V.S. at section office as to how long it took to inject 50 animals each. ~~This~~ In this manner an idea of how long the testing would take to complete. A rough estimate brought it up to a fortnight (roughly 5.800 animals)	
"	15.12.15	9 am	Section horses quite normal after injection	
"	16.12.15	9 am	8 sick animals evacuated from Steenwerck to Neuf Chatel	
"	17.12.15	11 am	Visited Div. Ammn. Col. to see a reported ~~case of~~ suspected reaction to mallein test. Decided to inject into the eye lid. D.D.V.S. afterwards called & said it was a highly suspicious reaction.	
"	18.12.15	12 am	Nothing of note	
"	19.12.15	1 pm	Received fourteen cases of shrapnel wounds. Two destroyed. All these animals were billeted in Armentieres	
"	20.12.15	9 pm	Held a P.M. on a horse which reacted to mallein test. Nodules, about twelve in number were found in lungs. The reaction in this case I should imagine typical. Eye nearly closed, lower lid hard & very painful with a muco-purulent discharge.	

4 · 33rd Mobile Vety. Section

WAR DIARY
or
INTELLIGENCE SUMMARY
(Erase heading not required.)

Army Form C. 2118

Instructions regarding War Diaries and Intelligence Summaries are contained in F. S. Regs., Part II. and the Staff Manual respectively. Title Pages will be prepared in manuscript.

Place	Date	Hour	Summary of Events and Information	Remarks and references to Appendices
NIEPPE	21.12.15	9 am	Vacated six animals from Steenwerck to Neuf Chatel	
"	22.12.15	10 am	Inspected 42 remounts which arrived for Division. Three cases of Ringworm discovered. About 50% of these horses were clipped.	
"	23.12.15	10 am	Visited 64 Field Ambulance. Reported shoeing of horses to C.O.	
		12 am	Received a complaint from R.T.O Steenwerck saying that L/Cpl. Rogers who proceeded to Neuf Chatel on 16 inst was missing from his truck at Hazebrouck + St. Omer Station. L/Cpl. Rogers statement was to the effect that at each of the stations he proceeded to other trucks on train to tie up horses owing to the men in these boxes being absent. He called as evidence train conductor.	
	24.12.15	9 am	Vacated 13 animals to Neuf Chatel.	
		2 pm	Inspected all horses of advanced section D.A.C. after being malleined on previous afternoon. No reactions	
	25/12/15	9 am.	Visited Claims Officer of Division re claims against section.	
		4 pm	Bathing parade for men.	

1875 Wt. W593/826 1,000,000 4/15 J.B.C. & A. A.D.S.S./Forms/C. 2118.

5

33 Mobile Vety. Section

Instructions regarding War Diaries and Intelligence Summaries are contained in F. S. Regs., Part II. and the Staff Manual respectively. Title Pages will be prepared in manuscript.

WAR DIARY
or
INTELLIGENCE SUMMARY
(Erase heading not required.)

Army Form C. 2118

Place	Date	Hour	Summary of Events and Information	Remarks and references to Appendices
Nieppe	26.12.15		Nothing of note	
"	27.12.15	8am	Proceeded to Strazeele to help to test horses of South Irish Horse	
"	28.12.15	10am	Visited waggon lines of 94 Bde R.F.A. There is a great improvement here as brick standings are being made	
"	29.12.15	4am 9am	Sergt Pegpert(?) of section proceeded to England on leave from Steenwerck Evacuated 7 horses from Steenwerck to Neuf Chatel. All bad mechanic(?) wounds.	
"	30.12.15	9am	Visited ordnance stores & Div Hd. Qrs.	
		2pm	Received a bad case of Pleurisy with effusion. Tapped chest – removed about a gallon of turbid lymph like fluid.	
	31.12.15	10am	Received eleven cases of shrapnel wounds from 94 Bde R.F.A. Horse which was tapped previous day decidedly better.	

Hogg Lawl(?)
OC 33 Mobile Vety Section

21st

33rd Indt: Ver: Sect:

Vol: 5

Jan '16

33 Mobile Vety. Section

Instructions regarding War Diaries and Intelligence Summaries are contained in F. S. Regs., Part II. and the Staff Manual respectively. Title Pages will be prepared in manuscript.

WAR DIARY
or
INTELLIGENCE SUMMARY

(Erase heading not required.)

Army Form C. 2118

Place	Date	Hour	Summary of Events and Information	Remarks and references to Appendices
NIEPPE	1/1/16	-	General holiday observed in section	
"	2/1/16	11 am	A.D.V.S. inspected section - sick on lines. Case of Tetanus admitted from 95 Bde R.F.A. This animal had eight shrapnel wounds on thorax received four days previous. Destroyed.	
	3/1/16	-		
		10 am	Vacated to Neuf-Berquin [?] 32 sick animals for Steenwerck. Mostly debilitated cases.	
	4.1.16	2.30 pm	D.D.V.S. 2nd Army visited section	
	5.1.16	12 am	Received one L.D. horse with suspected Mange. This animal had been dressed with some irritant ~~fluid~~ dressing probably paraffin on withers & quarters. Scrapings taken but no acari found.	
	6.1.16	12 am	Parade ~~of men~~ for Pont Nieppe Baths.	
		8 pm	Staff Sergeant Peaper [?] returned from leave having been 24 hours delayed in Boulogne at Rest Camp.	
	7.1.16	10 am	Vacated 25 sick animals for Steenwerck.	
	8.1.16	10 am	Collected 92 head collars from remounts arriving in Division. Some units are very slack regarding Div. orders on this subject.	J Hogg Capt AVC O.C. 33 Mob Vety Sec

33rd Mobile Vety. Section

WAR DIARY
or
INTELLIGENCE SUMMARY
(Erase heading not required.)

Army Form C. 2118

Instructions regarding War Diaries and Intelligence Summaries are contained in F. S. Regs., Part II. and the Staff Manual respectively. Title Pages will be prepared in manuscript.

Place	Date	Hour	Summary of Events and Information	Remarks and references to Appendices
NIEPPE	9.1.16	–	Nothing of note	
	10.1.16	10 am	~~Held~~ Gas helmet inspection & practice. Discovered four faulty helmets from badly fitting eye pieces. Visited 64 Field Ambulance. Several horses with lice including four later joined remounts.	
	11.1.16	12 am	Visited 64 Field Ambulance & advised lice cases to be clipped & washed	
	12.1.16	10 am	Evacuated 24 sick animals from Steenwerck to Neuf Chapelle	
	13.1.16	11 am	D.D.V.S. 2nd Army visited section	
		1 pm	Received 2 horses & 2 mules cast by D.D.R. 2nd Army.	
	14.1.16	–	Nothing of note	
	15.1.16	4 am	Proceeded on nine days leave England. Lieut Turner A.V.C. was ordered by A.D.V.S. Division to visit section each day to diagnose cases admitted for evacuation.	
			A.D.V.S. Division acted for me whilst on leave	
	16.1.16	11 am	Driver C. Lane A.S.C. acting as transport driver in section returned to unit as useless. Driver Smith taken on strength.	J. Hogg Capt. A.V.C. O.C. 33 Mob. Vety. Sect.

1875 Wt. W593/826 1,000,000 4/15 J.B.C. & A. A.D.S.S./Forms/C. 2118.

33rd Mobile Vety Section

Instructions regarding War Diaries and Intelligence Summaries are contained in F. S. Regs., Part II. and the Staff Manual respectively. Title Pages will be prepared in manuscript.

WAR DIARY
or
INTELLIGENCE SUMMARY
(Erase heading not required.)

Army Form C. 2118

Place	Date	Hour	Summary of Events and Information	Remarks and references to Appendices
NIEPPE	17.1.16	8 am	A great many shrapnel bullets fell in billets from British anti aircraft. Corp. Lewis proceeded to Paris by special permission S.H.Q. on 8 days leave. A.D.V.S. wrote to French Mission informing that Interpreter Poirson was three days absent after leave [illegible].	
"	18.1.16	9 am	Received orders from R.T.O. Steenwerck that no ~~one~~ sick animals could be evacuated for next four days on account of scarcity of trucks.	
"	19.1.16	–	Nothing of note	
"	20.1.16	10 am	Vacated 28 animals to Neuf-Chatel. This number included 4 suspected sarcoptic mange	
		3.30 pm	Sergt. Hardie A.V.C reported for duty from No.19 Vety. Hospital to take place of Sergt. Peapell promoted to Staff rank.	
"	21.1.16	2 pm	~~A~~D.D.V.S 2nd Army visited section. Advised clipping of all section horses. This was advocated last November.	
	22.1.16	3 am	Private Hart proceeded on leave for 8 days.	
		10 am	D.D.R 2nd Army inspected section horses.	
	23.1.16	9 am	Received three horses from 94 Bde R.F.A with confluent Ringworm. All horses clipped washed & when thoroughly dry calcium sulphide applied. ~~[illegible]~~ This was supposed to cure	[signature] Capt. A.V.C. O.C. 33 M.V.S.

1875 Wt. W593/826 1,000,000 4/15 J.B.C. & A. A.D.S.S./Forms/C. 2118.

Instructions regarding War Diaries and Intelligence Summaries are contained in F. S. Regs., Part II, and the Staff Manual respectively. Title Pages will be prepared in manuscript.

Army Form C. 2118.

WAR DIARY
or
INTELLIGENCE SUMMARY
(Erase heading not required).

Place	Date	Hour	Summary of Events and Information	Remarks and references to Appendices
	Continued			
NIEPPE	23.1.16		ringworm in ~~the~~ the dressing but failed in these cases.	
	24.1.16	3 am	Arrived back from leave. Received official information of promotion to Captain	
		11 am	Visited ^inspected^ Hd. Qrs. Chargers. Have ^had^ reported to complain of shoeing of these animals	
	25.1.16	3 am	Major McDonald (A.D.V.S.) proceeded on leave for 10 days & ordered me to act for him in his place	
		11 am	Visited office of A.D.V.S. ARMENTIERES	
		4 pm	Staff-Sergt. Peaden A.V.C. proceeded to No. 19 Hospital. This N.C.O. has been with this section since its formation & has given every satisfaction.	
	26.1.16	9 am	Visited office A.D.V.S.	
		10 am	Visited Div. Amm. Col. regarding suspicious reaction to Mallein test. Found a large probably septic swelling	
	27.1.16	9 am	Visited 94 Ammun. Column. Found animals looking very well & a great improvement in condition of standings.	D. Hogg Capt. A.V.C. O.C. 33 M.V.S.

BSD - B. M351/22/11. 12/15. 5000.

33rd Mobile Vety Section.

Instructions regarding War Diaries and Intelligence Summaries are contained in F. S. Regs., Part II, and the Staff Manual respectively. Title Pages will be prepared in manuscript.

WAR DIARY
or
INTELLIGENCE SUMMARY
(Erase heading not required).

Army Form C. 2118.

Place	Date	Hour	Summary of Events and Information	Remarks and references to Appendices
NIEPPE	28.1.16	9am	Vacated 24 sick animals Neuf Chatel. The greater majority of these were young debilitated horses. The ration of hay (6 lbs) is quickly showing itself. I have gone carefully into the rations received by me + it works out about 4½ – 5 lbs of hay per day.	
	29.1.16	10am	Visited ordnance regarding horse shoes recently received in section. The nail holes of these shoes are very bad being very coarse.	
		2 pm.	Tube helmet parade – practice	
	30.1.16	9am	Visited 94 Ammn Column. These horses are falling off in condition	
		12am	Bathing parade of men at Pont Nieppe baths.	
			Visited Hd. Qrs.	
	31.1.16	10 am.	Vacated 16 animals to Neuf-Chatel	
		11.30 am	Received 8 horses with shrapnel wounds from ARMENTIERS	
		3 pm		

D Hogg Capt AVC
OC 33 M.V.S.

BSD - B. M351/22/11. 12/15. 5000.

33 M.V.S.
21st Div
Vol. 6.

33 Mobile Vety Section

Instructions regarding War Diaries and Intelligence Summaries are contained in F. S. Regs., Part II, and the Staff Manual respectively. Title Pages will be prepared in manuscript.

WAR DIARY
or
INTELLIGENCE SUMMARY
(Erase heading not required).

Army Form C. 2118.

Place	Date	Hour	Summary of Events and Information	Remarks and references to Appendices
NIEPPE	1.2.16	10 am	Visited Div. Ammn. Col. to inspect 40 mules recently arrived (acting for ADVS Div) These mules were excellent in condition & of good stamp	
	2.2.16	9 am	Evacuated 16 horses from Steenwerck to Neuf-Chatel. These were all cases of debility	
		6 pm	Issued 3 mules which had been found straying near Mallin	
		11.30 pm	Called to Pont de NIEPPE to see two horses which had bolted & got into the river. One horse died before I got there. Other horse inject. Strychnine & recovered in 2 hrs	
	3.2.16	9 am	Evacuated 19 animals from Steenwerck (3 suspected sarcoptic mange cases)	
	4.2.16	4.30 am	Dispatched N.C.O. & man to TOUVANNE [?] to bring back a horse ambulance in place of the one G.S. limbered waggon	
		2 pm	Visited St. Jan's Cappel to see 2 cases suspected mange. Scrapings negative	
	5.2.16	3 pm	Collected head collars of Div. Ammn. animals at Steenwerck. 92 in number	
		4 pm	Dispatched two chargers General Dorothin-Walker [?], which had been placed in my charge, to England	
	6.2.16	9 am	Evacuated 16 animals to Neuf Chatel.	
		1 pm	Visited 64 Field Ambulance & sent two H.D. horses into M.V. Section	[signature illegible] Capt A.V.C. O.C. 33 M.V. Sect

BSD - B. M351/22/14. 12/15. 5000.

33rd Mobile Vety Section

Instructions regarding War Diaries and Intelligence Summaries are contained in F. S. Regs., Part II, and the Staff Manual respectively. Title Pages will be prepared in manuscript.

WAR DIARY
or
INTELLIGENCE SUMMARY
(Erase heading not required).

Army Form C. 2118.

Place	Date	Hour	Summary of Events and Information	Remarks and references to Appendices
NIEPPE	7.2.16	9 am	Vaccd 10 horses Neuf Chateau [illegible]	
		4 pm	N.C.O. returned from TOURNAI [illegible]	
			ABBEVILLE [illegible] four days.	
		4.30 pm	Visited 95 Bde R.F.A. to inspect [illegible]	
	8.2.16	10 am	Exchanged [illegible] gas helmets for a fresh issue. All helmets with [illegible] eye pieces ~~[illegible]~~ returned to Stores.	
		2.30 pm	3 cases shrapnel wounds admitted. [illegible] All [illegible] ARMENTIERES.	
	9.2.16	9 am	Collected 2 horses from [illegible] near BAILLEUL [illegible] Canadian Division	
		2 pm	NIEPPE shelled [illegible] uncomfortably close to Section billets	
		4 pm	Received [illegible] boarding for [illegible] standings for 62nd Inf. Bde. [illegible]	
	10.2.16	11 am	Cd. [illegible] A.A. [illegible] visited section	
		2.30 pm	Visited [illegible] Field Ambulance, 95 Bde RFA (C Batty) [illegible]	
	11.2.16	12 am	D.D.V.S. 2nd Army visited section. Expressed satisfaction.	
	12.2.16	9 am	Evacuated 16 animals. Visited 95 Bde (C Batty). ~~[illegible]~~ [illegible] acting in place of Lt. [illegible] A.V.C. indisposed	[illegible] Capt. [illegible]

BSD - B. M351/22/11. 12/15. 5000.

33 Mobile Vety Section

Instructions regarding War Diaries and Intelligence Summaries are contained in F. S. Regs., Part II, and the Staff Manual respectively. Title Pages will be prepared in manuscript.

WAR DIARY
or
INTELLIGENCE SUMMARY
(Erase heading not required).

Army Form C. 2118.

Place	Date	Hour	Summary of Events and Information	Remarks and references to Appendices
			continued	
NIEPPE	12/2/16	2 pm	Horse ambulance (R.S.P.C.A) ~~model~~ arrived. On bad roads I should think the axle too near ground + curved rods back + front are bound to come into contact with ground. The ~~[illegible]~~ method of harnessing two horses abreast is impossible for the narrow roads of this district	
	13/2/16		Nothing of note	
	14/2/16	9 am	Boxed 19 sick animals to Neufchatel	
		11 am	Visited Hd Qrs (Div.) to interview C.R.E. re covered standings for sick horses. Erection of these promised as soon as necessary material arrives	
	15/2/16	8.30 am	Left Bailleul with A.D.V.S. to proceed to Neufchatel to visit Base Vety Hospitals	
Neufchatel	15/2/16	11.30 am	arrived Neufchatel	
		2.30	Inspected No. 12 Hospital.	
		3.15	" " 13 Hospital	
		4	# .. Mange hospital	
			Every thing highly satisfactory + arrangements for dealing with animals excellent.	
	16/2/16	10.30 a.m.	Inspected No. 3 Vety Hospital near Boulogne.	

J Hogg
Capt. A.V.C.

BSD - B. M351/22/11. 12/15. 5000.

33 Mobile Vety. Section

Instructions regarding War Diaries and Intelligence Summaries are contained in F. S. Regs., Part II, and the Staff Manual respectively. Title Pages will be prepared in manuscript.

WAR DIARY
or
INTELLIGENCE SUMMARY
(Erase heading not required).

Army Form C. 2118.

Place	Date	Hour	Summary of Events and Information	Remarks and references to Appendices
NIEPPE	17.2.16	9 a.m.	Visited all Batteries of 95 Bde RFA also animals of 63rd Inf. Bde	
"		11 am	acting (D.D.VS 2nd Army called & inspected section. He asked for a report on the horse ambulance re improvements in harness, grouping of team, & improvements to vehicle.	
"	18.2.16	9 am	Vacated 18 animals from Steenwerck.	
	19.2.16	12 am	Received 9 cases of Shrapnel wounds from Hospitals. The majority of these after treatment will be sent back to units.	
		2 am	Visited 64 Field Ambulance.	
"	20.2.16	9 am	Vacated 13 animals (sick) from Steenwerck Mostly debility. Most of these cases to put down to reduced hay ration.	
"	21.2.16	10 am	Received 8 skin scrapings from suspected mange case 97 Bde R.F.A. Sarcoptic parasite found in one & Symbiotic in three. [struck through]	
		4 pm	Received drugs from base stores. There seems to be great difficulty in procuring bandages here.	
	22.2.16	—	Nothing of note	[signature] Capt. A.V.C.

BSD - B. M851 22/11. 12/15. 5000.

Instructions regarding War Diaries and Intelligence Summaries are contained in F. S. Regs., Part II, and the Staff Manual respectively. Title Pages will be prepared in manuscript.

WAR DIARY
or
INTELLIGENCE SUMMARY
(Erase heading not required).

Army Form C. 2118.

Place	Date	Hour	Summary of Events and Information	Remarks and references to Appendices
NIEPPE	22.2.16	10 am	Collected 97 lead collars for [summers?] arriving. Certificate sent to D.D.R. 2nd Army.	
"	23.2.16	9 am	Vaccinated 16 animals Steenwerck (this number included 8 suspected mange cases)	
	24.2.16	10 am	Ordered to build Dug-out behind horse lines. Drew materials from C.R.E. & completed same by evening.	
	25.2.16	9 am.	Nothing of note	
	26.2.16	10 am	Visited Field Remount section near CAESTRE to draw [clips?] for self	
		2 pm.	D.D.V.S. 2nd Army visited section	
	27.2.16	9 am.	Vaccinated 8 suspected mange cases	
	28.2.16	10 am	Visited D.A.C at St. Jans Cappel. A number of itching horses were reported but mostly due to lice.	
	29.2.16	—	Nothing of note	[illegible] Capt AVC

BSD - B. M351/22/14. 12/15. 5000.

93 M Vet S
Vol 7

33 Mobile Vety Section

WAR DIARY
or
INTELLIGENCE SUMMARY.
(Erase heading not required.)

Army Form C. 2118.

Instructions regarding War Diaries and Intelligence Summaries are contained in F. S. Regs., Part II. and the Staff Manual respectively. Title pages will be prepared in manuscript.

Place	Date	Hour	Summary of Events and Information	Remarks and references to Appendices
NIEPPE	1.3.16	9am	Vacated 14 sick animals NEUF-CHATEL. Included six suspected sarcoptic mange cases.	
"	2.3.16	10am	Visited 64 Field ambulance & sent two horses to M.V.S.	
"	3.3.16	9am	Vacated 17 sick animals included 2 susp. mange cases. Parade of section for Divisional baths.	
"		2pm	Harness & saddle inspection	
"	4.3.16	11am	A.D.V.S. inspected section horses & transport.	
		6pm	Visited 94 Bde R.F.A. to collect ~~Hd.~~ collars of 34 animals for division	
	5.3.16		Nothing of note	
	6.3.16	10am	Visited C.R.E. to make arrangements for weekly supply of lime for preparation of calcium for Division	
		2pm	Visited 63 & 64 Field ambulances. In both ~~cases~~ reported to A.D.V.S of bad shoeing.	
	7.3.16	11am	D.D.V.S. 2nd Army visited section	
		2pm	Visited abattoir at NIEPPE with D.D.V.S 2nd Army. The French system of meat inspection I think poor & open in many	

33rd Mobile Vety. Section

Instructions regarding War Diaries and Intelligence Summaries are contained in F. S. Regs., Part II. and the Staff Manual respectively. Title pages will be prepared in manuscript.

WAR DIARY
or
INTELLIGENCE SUMMARY.
(Erase heading not required.)

Army Form C. 2118.

Place	Date	Hour	Summary of Events and Information	Remarks and references to Appendices
			Continued	
NIEPPE			way to be evacuated	
"	8.3.16	12am	Evacuated 18 animals NEUF CHATEL. Included 3 mange cases	
"	9.3.16	9am	Evacuated 13 animals.	
"		2pm	Visited abbatoir at Bailleul with D.D.V.S. 2nd Army. Here again system poor.	
"	10.3.16	11am	Visited Hd. Qrs ARMENTIERES. Reported to A.D.V.S. a suspicious reaction to mallein test.	
	11.3.16	9am	Admitted re charger with Tetanus. This animal had been wounded with Shrapnel 14 days previous. Injected 3000 anti tetanic serum with laxative medicine	
	12.3.16	10am	Inspected all Hd. Qrs. Staff horses	
		2pm	As acting A.D.V.S. accompanied Div. General in inspection of Infantry transport	
	13.3.16	10am	Visited 95 Bde R.F.A. A.C. to inspect recently received remounts. These are L.D. horses of a bad type. [illegible] poor.	
	14.3.16	9am	Evacuated 24 horses to NEUF-CHATEL. Included 3 suspected mange cases	
	15.3.16	9am	Evac. 15 animals NEUF-CHATEL.	

33 Mob. Vety. Section

WAR DIARY
or
INTELLIGENCE SUMMARY.
(*Erase heading not required.*)

Army Form C. 2118.

Instructions regarding War Diaries and Intelligence Summaries are contained in F. S. Regs., Part II. and the Staff Manual respectively. Title pages will be prepared in manuscript. ~~England~~

Place	Date	Hour	Summary of Events and Information	Remarks and references to Appendices
NIEPPE ~~15.3.16~~	15.3.16	2 pm	Visited billets of Mob. Vety. Sec. of 17 Div. & arranged with O.C. to take over from him when Division moved. This is a poor billet, with no cover for horses & water supply bad. Housing for men fair.	
"	16.3.16		Nothing of note	
"	17.3.16	10 am	Received three cases shrapnel wounds from ARMENTIERS. One case showed severe injuries to both eyes. Destroyed.	
"	18.3.16	9 am	Vacated 18 animals NEUF-CHATEL. Included 4 mange cases. Received 480 gas helmets horse for distribution 10/ to each unit	
"	19.3.16		Nothing of note	
"	20.3.16	9 am	Vacated 24 sick animals NEUF CHATEL	
		11 am	Received movement orders for Divisional move	
		3 pm	Packed limbered wagon to accompany advance party.	
"	21.3.16	10 am	Advance party of 1 Corporal 2 men with limbered wagon left for CAESTRE. Loaded both remaining wagons ready to move	
"	22.3.16	8 am	Main party left for CAESTRE. On journey evacuated 16 animals at Steenwerck	

T2134. Wt. W708—776. 500000. 4/15. Sir J. C. & S.

33 Mobile Vety Section

Instructions regarding War Diaries and Intelligence Summaries are contained in F. S. Regs., Part II. and the Staff Manual respectively. Title pages will be prepared in manuscript.

WAR DIARY
or
INTELLIGENCE SUMMARY.
(Erase heading not required.)

Army Form C. 2118.

Place	Date	Hour	Summary of Events and Information	Remarks and references to Appendices
CAESTRE	23.3.16	3.45 pm	Placed Sergt J. Leitch of Section under open arrest for absence without leave whilst on duty.	
"	24.3.16	10 am	Remanded Sergt Leitch for 24 hrs.	
		2 pm	Visited 65 Field ambulance & returned two horses into M. V. Sect.	
"	25.3.16	10 am	Sergt Leitch A.V.C severely reprimanded	
		3 pm	Evac. 24 animals from CAESTRE	
"	26.3.16	7 am	Dispatched a corporal & one man to R.T.O. St. Omer by order of D.D.V.S 2 Army to conduct sick horses to Base Hospital	
"	27.3.16	3 pm	Evacuated 17 animals NEUF-CHATEL	
"	28.3.16	2 pm	Movement orders for entraining with Division received	
"	29.3.16	2 pm	Visited 65 Field ambulance & 75 Bde RFA A.C	
"	30.3.16	3 pm	Vacated 16 animals NEUF-CHATEL	
		10 pm	Visited Hd. Qrs. Div Train. Horse inflam bowels	
	31.3.16	3 pm	Vacated 24 animals NEUF-CHATEL included 4 mange	

J. Hogg Capt A.V.C
O.C. 33 Mob Vety Sect.

T2134. Wt. W708—776. 500000. 4/15. Sir J. C. & S.

33 Mobile Vety Section

Instructions regarding War Diaries and Intelligence Summaries are contained in F. S. Regs., Part II. and the Staff Manual respectively. Title pages will be prepared in manuscript.

WAR DIARY
or
INTELLIGENCE SUMMARY.
(Erase heading not required.)

Army Form C. 2118.

33 M Vet Sec
Vol 8

Place	Date	Hour	Summary of Events and Information	Remarks and references to Appendices
~~[illegible]~~ Caestre	1.4.16	11am	Vacated 15 animals NEUF-CHATEL	
	.		Completed packing of vehicles in view of move	
	.	3 pm	moved off with section to entrain	
	.	4.40 pm	arrived GODEWAERSVELDE station & reported to R.T.O.	
		6 pm	Began entrainment which took ¾ hour	
	~~2.4.16~~	8 pm	Train left GODEWAERSVELDE	
	2.4.16	7 am	arrived at AMIENS. All horses travelled well.	
		7.45 am	Left for Ribemont. The journey taking five hours. Billets good.	
RIBEMONT	2.4.16	9 am	Received 8 horses injured in journey South. A great amount of work needed to make billets inhabitable especially as regards sanitary arrangements.	
	3.4.16	10 am	Inspected all Hd. Qr. (Div) Chargers & Transport	
		2 pm	Inspected horses Div. Signal Coy.	
	4.4.16	12 pm	A.D.V.S. 4 Army inspected section & expressed satisfaction	
	5.4.16		Nothing of note	
	6.4.16	10 pm	Received 5 cases of shell wounds in horse from MEAULTE. One case destroyed	

T2134. Wt. W708—776. 500000. 4/15. Sir J. C. & S.

33 Mobile Vety. Section

Instructions regarding War Diaries and Intelligence Summaries are contained in F. S. Regs., Part II. and the Staff Manual respectively. Title pages will be prepared in manuscript.

WAR DIARY
or
INTELLIGENCE SUMMARY.
(Erase heading not required.)

Army Form C. 2118.

Place	Date	Hour	Summary of Events and Information	Remarks and references to Appendices
Ribemont	7.4.16	10am	Received four horses susp. mange from 94 Bde R.F.A. No acari found microscopically	
		2pm	Inspected A Squad. South Irish Horse. These horses have poor condition of [illegible]	
	8.4.16	9am	Received three susp. mange + 2 stragglers cases. Both latter cases claimed for Remounts	
	9.4.16		Nothing of note	
	10.4.16	11am	Evacuated 16 horses. Included 3 susp mange. Acari found in one case	
	11.4.16	9am	Visited 65 Field Ambulance. Sent in 4 horses to Mob Vety Sect	
	12.4.16	10am	Visited 65 Field Ambulance + South Irish Horse. The horses of latter are still poor in condition	
	13.4.16	11am	Evacuated 12 sick animals. Included 4 susp mange	
	14.4.16	9am	Collected Hd. collars of 32 Remounts issued to Division	
		11am	Inspected all Div Hd Qrs. Chargers	
	15.4.16	9am	Received three horses wounded by shell fire from MEAULTE	
	16.4.16	11am	Visited VILLE: surrounding district with A.D.V.S. of Div to arrange for place for advanced dressing station. Decided on place in meadow of artillery wagon lines	

33 Mob Vety Section

Instructions regarding War Diaries and Intelligence Summaries are contained in F. S. Regs., Part II, and the Staff Manual respectively. Title pages will be prepared in manuscript.

WAR DIARY
or
INTELLIGENCE SUMMARY.
(*Erase heading not required.*)

Army Form C. 2118.

Place	Date	Hour	Summary of Events and Information	Remarks and references to Appendices
RIBEMONT	17.4.16	11am	Vacated 16 animals to ABBEVILLE	
"	18.4.16		Nothing of note	
"	19.4.16	10am	Received 2 susp mange cases fr 97 Bde RFA. Acari found in one case	
"	20.4.16	9am	Visited CORBIE to purchase lime for preparation of Calcium Sulphide for whole Division	
"	21.4.16	12am	General [illegible] Div. Commander visited section & expressed satisfaction	
"	22.4.16	11am	Vacated 16 animals to ABBEVILLE. Included 2 susp mange	
"	23.4.16	9am	Visited 63 Field Ambulance. Complained to O.C. of bad shoeing	
"	24.4.16	10am	Received three [illegible] fr HdQrs 94 Bde. Extremely itchy. Found acari (sarcoptic) in two cases.	
"	25.4.16	10am	Inspected S.S. Horse. Inspected forage found it of extremely bad quality. Oats of fair sample but extremely dirty. Hay [illegible] good. Sent complaint to ADOS of Div	
"	26.4.16	3pm	DDVS of 4 Army visited Section	
"	27.4.16		Visited 64 Field Ambulance. Paraded all horses	

T2134. Wt. W708—776. 500000. 4/15. Sir J. C. & S.

33 Mob. Vety. Section

Instructions regarding War Diaries and Intelligence Summaries are contained in F. S. Regs., Part II. and the Staff Manual respectively. Title pages will be prepared in manuscript.

WAR DIARY
or
INTELLIGENCE SUMMARY.
(Erase heading not required.)

Army Form C. 2118.

Place	Date	Hour	Summary of Events and Information	Remarks and references to Appendices
RIBEMONT	28.4.16	11 am	Visited BONNAY (No 3 Sect A.S.C) The majority of animals here have lice. In 8 cases I ordered clipping, the majority of others I sprayed with 1–50 Nicotine	
	29.4.16	11 am	Evacuated 16 animals to ABBEVILLE. Included 3 mange cases	
	30.4.16	10 am	Visited 65 Field Ambulance & S.J. Horse. The horses of latter unit are improving	

D. Hogg Capt
A.V.C

O.C. 33 Mob. Vety Section

T2134. Wt. W708–776. 500000. 4/15. Sir J. C. & S.

33 Mobile Vety Section

33 M Vet Sec

(21)

Vol 9

Instructions regarding War Diaries and Intelligence Summaries are contained in F. S. Regs., Part II. and the Staff Manual respectively. Title pages will be prepared in manuscript.

Army Form C. 2118.

WAR DIARY or INTELLIGENCE SUMMARY.

(Erase heading not required.)

Place	Date	Hour	Summary of Events and Information	Remarks and references to Appendices
RIBEMONT	1.5.16	9am	82 Remounts received for Division. Collected head collars of same	
			Pte. Hodge reports loss of pay book	
	2.5.16	10am	Distributed Gas helmets horse to all units	
		3pm	Vacated 32 sick animals Included 4 susp. Sarcoptic mange cases	
	3.5.16	10am	Held inspection of all Hd Qrs Div. Chargers	
		2pm	visited 62 Field ambulance. Ordered two horses into M.V. Section	
	4.5.16		Nothing of note	
	5.5.16	3pm	Vacated 24 animals to ABBEVILLE	
		4pm	Section men attended Div. baths	
	6.5.16	11am	Went with A.D.V.S. to make final arrangements re advanced Section at Dernancourt.	
	7.5.16	8am	Went with 1 corporal & 5 men to site for advanced section. Erected lines, water troughs etc	
		3pm	Visited 63 Field ambulance & 21 Signal Coy	
	8.5.16	9am	Drew 1810 Fr. from Field Paymaster at HEILLY for Section pay	
		2pm	Visited 125 Heavy Batty R.G.A.	

T2134. Wt. W708—776. 500000. 4/15. Sir J. C. & S.

33 Mobile Vety Section

Instructions regarding War Diaries and Intelligence Summaries are contained in F. S. Regs., Part II. and the Staff Manual respectively. Title pages will be prepared in manuscript.

WAR DIARY
or
INTELLIGENCE SUMMARY.
(Erase heading not required.)

Army Form C. 2118.

Place	Date	Hour	Summary of Events and Information	Remarks and references to Appendices
RIBEMONT	9.5.16	9 am	Visited 65 Field ambulance.	
	10.5.16	10 am	32 Remounts received in Division. Head collars collected	
	11.5.16	8 am	Visited 125 & 130 ~~Heavy~~ Batty R.G.A. Six horses sent into M.V. Sect.	
		2 pm	Visited advanced M.V. Section	
	12.5.16	3 pm	Evac. 18 animals ABBEVILLE. Including 2 mange	
	13.5.16	10 am	Inspected 21 Div. Signal animals. These animals (sheet?) looking poor	
	14.5.16	8 am	Departed for ABBEVILLE to look around Vety. Hospitals there	
ABBEVILLE		3 pm	arrived ABBEVILLE reporting immediately to D.V.S	
		5 pm	Visited no. 22 Hospital	
	15.5.16	9 am	Visited hospitals commanded by Majors Shepherd – Wadley	
	"	4 pm	Departed for RIBEMONT	
RIBEMONT	16.5.16	10 am	Handed over Vety. charge of 125 130 Batty R.G.A. to Capt. Tindell	
	17.5.16	11 am	Placed Sergt. Hardie under arrest for galloping section horse. This N.C.O. has been under observation for some time but no definite charge could be brought against him. I brought certain evidence against him this morning & he admitted offence.	

33 Mobile Vety Section

WAR DIARY
or
INTELLIGENCE SUMMARY.
(Erase heading not required.)

Army Form C. 2118.

Instructions regarding War Diaries and Intelligence Summaries are contained in F. S. Regs., Part II. and the Staff Manual respectively. Title pages will be prepared in manuscript.

Place	Date	Hour	Summary of Events and Information	Remarks and references to Appendices
RIBEMONT	18.5.16	9am	Brought Sergt Hardie before Major McDonald. Offence disobeying an order. The N.C.O. pleaded guilty. Remanded for 24 hrs.	
		2pm	Received letter from A.Q.M.G. 21 Div. for office	
"	19.5.16	9am	Sergt. Hardie reduced to rank of private. Corporal Cross made acting Sergeant. L/Cpl. Lowe promoted Corporal.	
"	20.5.16		Nothing of note	
"	21.5.16	10am	11 Remounts arrived. Head collars collected	
"	22.5.16	2pm	Visited 63 64 65 Field ambulances	
		4pm	advanced section. 8 cases shrapnel wounds received here today	
"	23.5.16	3pm	Evacuated 8 sick animals ABBEVILLE	
		4pm	Received 1000 Fr. for section pay from Field cashier	
"	24.5.16	2pm	Sergt Leinster evacuated to Havre to undergo dental treatment	
		3pm	Went to HEILLY to meet Lieut Wall AVC reporting to Division	
"	25.5.16	2pm	Pte Hardie dispatched No. 2 Vety Hospital HAVRE	
"	26.5.16	2pm	Evacuated 16 horses ABBEVILLE	
			Cpl. Parker late clerk to ADVS reports ~~attached~~ to section for duty. Authority Base Records	

T2134. Wt. W708—776. 500000. 4/15. Sir J. C. & S.

33 Mobile Vety. Section

Army Form C. 2118.

WAR DIARY
or
INTELLIGENCE SUMMARY.
(Erase heading not required.)

Instructions regarding War Diaries and Intelligence Summaries are contained in F. S. Regs., Part II. and the Staff Manual respectively. Title pages will be prepared in manuscript.

Place	Date	Hour	Summary of Events and Information	Remarks and references to Appendices
RIBEMONT ~~[illegible]~~	27.5.16	7am	Sergt. Harrison reports fr No. 2 Vety Hospital in place of Sergt. Hardie	
	28.5.16	9am	Inspected all Hd Qr Staff chargers	
	29.5.16	9am	Received 8 cases of Shrapnel was injured at MEAULT on previous night	
	30.5.16	10am	Visited advanced Section	
		4p	visited 63 · 65 Field ambulances.	
	31.5.16	10am	A field of grass handed over by Supply Officer to be cut for Section horses	
		2pm	D.D.V.S. 4th Army visited Section	

J Hogg Capt AVC
OC 33 Mob. Vety Section

T2134. Wt. W708—776. 500000. 4/15. Sir J. C. & S.

33 Mob. Vety. S[redacted]ion

Instructions regarding War Diaries and Intelligence Summaries are contained in F. S. Regs., Part II. and the Staff Manual respectively. Title pages will be prepared in manuscript.

WAR DIARY
or
INTELLIGENCE SUMMARY.
(Erase heading not required.)

~~BM~~ 21 JUNE

Army Form C. 2118.

33 M Vet Sec

VOL 10

Place	Date	Hour	Summary of Events and Information	Remarks and references to Appendices
RUBEMPRE ~~H~~	1/6/16	8.30am	Proceeded on leave for 8 days to U.K. Handed over section to A.D.V.S.	
"	2/6/16	10am	3 suspect mange cases arrived. Scrapings exam by Lieut. Ging AVC Negative	
			Major McDonald visited advanced section	
"	3/6/16	6am	Horse dispatched 9 KOYLI. for one mule - Pneumonia	
		10am	No 618 Sergt. E James arrived at section from HAVRE in place of Sergt Hardie reduced to Private	
	4/6/16	2pm	Vacated 20 sick animals to FORGES - les - Eaux	
		6pm	Susp. case of glanders arrived. Mallein at 9 pm. Intra-palpebral test	
	5/6/16	9pm	Collected three shrapnel cases from MEAULTE	
		6pm	Received 9 sick horses into section	
		9pm	No reaction to horse mallein on previous night	
	6/6/16	8am	Destroyed two horses - shrapnel wounds	
		10am	Sent horse to BRESLE to fetch horse of 15 Royal Scots	
	7/6/16	4pm	68 remounts arrived for Division. One case of strangles + two sarcoptic mange cases in batch. This is the third time in succession that susp. cases of mange have arrived with remounts	

T2134. Wt. W708—776. 500000. 4/15. Sir J. C. & S.

33rd M/16. Vety. Section

Army Form C. 2118.

Instructions regarding War Diaries and Intelligence Summaries are contained in F. S. Regs., Part II. and the Staff Manual respectively. Title pages will be prepared in manuscript.

WAR DIARY
or
INTELLIGENCE SUMMARY.
(Erase heading not required.)

Place	Date	Hour	Summary of Events and Information	Remarks and references to Appendices
RIBEMONT	8/6/16	—	Nothing of note	
"	9/6/16	9am	7 sick animals admitted	
		2pm	Ambulance sent to 95 Bde R.F.A	
"	10/6/16	6pm	Fatigues sent to line pit to bring line for completion of roadway in section	
"	11/6/16	6pm	Returned from leave	
"	12/6/16	8am	Visited & inspected all Hd. Qrs. Chargers	
		1pm	Visited 64 Field Ambulance. 2 lame cases sent to M.V. Section	
"	13/6/16	9am	Inspected 21 Div. Signal Horses. These horses are improving in condition but are dirty from lack of grooming. I impressed on Officer in Charge each time I visit but there seems to be no method of supervision	
"	14/6/16	2pm	Vacated 27 sick animals including 4 mange to ABBEVILLE	
"	15/6/16	—	Nothing of note	
"	16/6/16	9am	Visited 21 Div Sigs. Sent two horses into M.V.S.	
		2pm	Inspect. all horses of 63rd Field Ambulance. Animals in good condition	
	17/6/16	9am	4 Susp. mange cases arrived. Scrapings negative	

T2134. Wt. W708–776. 500000. 4/15. Sir J. C. & S.

33 Mob. Vety Section

Instructions regarding War Diaries and Intelligence Summaries are contained in F. S. Regs., Part II. and the Staff Manual respectively. Title pages will be prepared in manuscript.

WAR DIARY
or
INTELLIGENCE SUMMARY.
(Erase heading not required.)

Army Form C. 2118.

Place	Date	Hour	Summary of Events and Information	Remarks and references to Appendices
RIBEMONT	18.6.16	9am	Collected 5 sick animals R.F.A. wagon lines	
		11am	Susp mange case admitted fr A/95 Bde R.F.A. Three scrapings taken + in each acari were found.	
"	19.6.16	12pm	Evacuated 32 sick animals ABBEVILLE. Included 3 mange.	
"		6pm	Visited 64 Field Ambulance	
"	20.6.16		Nothing of note	
"	21.6.16	9pm	Mallein (intra palpebral) three riding cobs 62nd Inf. Bde	
"	22.6.16	12pm	Vaccinated 32 sick animals. Including 8 mange	
		9pm	Results of previous days inoculation negative	
"	23.6.16	9am	Inspected 21 Div. Signal horses	
		11am	Collected three ambulance cases (shrapnel) fr MEAULTE	
"	24.6.16	10am	Conference of V.O's of Division held	
		10.30am	47 Remounts arrived fr Division. Head collars collected. one mange case isolated	
"	25.6.16	12am	Vaccinated 20 sick animals FORGES-les-EAUX	
			Received drugs for section, + Divisional ~~HQ~~ QD.	

33rd Mob. Vety. Section

Instructions regarding War Diaries and Intelligence Summaries are contained in F. S. Regs., Part II. and the Staff Manual respectively. Title pages will be prepared in manuscript.

WAR DIARY
or
INTELLIGENCE SUMMARY.
(Erase heading not required.)

Army Form C. 2118.

Place	Date	Hour	Summary of Events and Information	Remarks and references to Appendices
RIBEMONT	26.6.16	10 am	ADVS inspected section	
		12 am	accompanied A.D.V.S during inspection of 96 Bde R.F.A.	
		4 pm	Received 12 animals into section	
"	27.6.16	10 am	Visited Field Remount section 4 Army to draw clayer for seef	
"		2 pm	visited by order of ADVS 3 civilian horses injured by shell fire	
"	28.6.16	12 pm	Vacated 18 sick animals FORGES-LES-EAUX	
"	29.6.16	10 am	visited Infantry wagon lines with ADVS during the inspection of Infantry transport	
"	30.6.16	12 am	Evacuated 22 animals including 3 cases mange	
		2 pm	visited 21 Div. Sigs. horses also 64 Field ambulance	

J. Hogg Capt AVC
OC 33 Mob. Vety. Sect.

T2134. Wt. W708—776. 500000. 4/15. Sir J. C. & S.

D.A.A. & Q.M.G.
21 Division

Herewith diary for July
Please

J. Hogg
Capt. A.V.C.
30. 7. 16

O.C. 33 Mob. Vety. Sect.

33rd Mob Vety. Section **WAR DIARY** *or* **INTELLIGENCE SUMMARY.** *(Erase heading not required.)*

21 July

Army Form C. 2118.

33 M Vet Sec

Vol //

Instructions regarding War Diaries and Intelligence Summaries are contained in F. S. Regs., Part II. and the Staff Manual respectively. Title pages will be prepared in manuscript.

Place	Date	Hour	Summary of Events and Information	Remarks and references to Appendices
RIBEMONT	1/7/16	9am	Received three suspect mange cases from 95 Bde RFA. Microscopic exam failed to reveal Sarcoptes	
		2pm	Evacuated 24 sick animals from MERICOURT. This included 4 susp mange	
			Received telegram re remounts due at MERICOURT at 11.55pm. Paraded one N.C.O. & six men for the collecting. Train did not arrive until 6.30 am. Seventy two remounts arrived. The horses were very poor but L.D. mules which replaced L.D. horses were good. Segregated 3 H.D. horses from batch which were itchy	
"	2/7/16	9am	visited ~~Hd~~ Qr. Charges & paraded all horses of 21 Div. Sigs. The latter horses are improving in condition but are still dirty. The bad grooming is due to lack of supervision	
"	3/7/16	2pm	Evacuated 19 animals including three mange. Visited artillery waggon lines with A.D.V.S. & arranged moving of advanced section. ~~This~~	
		9pm	advanced section arrived at waggon lines	
	4/7/16	3am	Reveille. Completed packing at 6am	
		6.30am	Left RIBEMONT for Ailly-sur-SOMME arriving after a good journey at 3 p.m. Found good standing for horses & good place for men	
Ailly-sur-SOMME	5/7/16	10am	Received seven surgical cases for evacuation	
		9pm	Mallained one H.D. horse of 95 BDE RFA with chronic nasal discharge	

T2134. Wt. W708-776. 500000. 4/15. Sir J. C. & S.

33 Mobile Vety Section

Instructions regarding War Diaries and Intelligence Summaries are contained in F. S. Regs., Part II. and the Staff Manual respectively. Title pages will be prepared in manuscript.

WAR DIARY
or
INTELLIGENCE SUMMARY.
(Erase heading not required.)

Army Form C. 2118.

Place	Date	Hour	Summary of Events and Information	Remarks and references to Appendices
Ailly-sur-Somme	6/7/16	2 pm	Received horse from 64 Field ambulance. Itchy. Found sarcoptic parasite in skin scrapings. From information received this animal had only shown itchyness for 24 hrs.	
"	"	5 pm	Received orders to move to CAVILLON on following day.	
"	7/7/16	9.30	Left with convoy & arrived after 2½ hrs. journey at billet in Bois de CAVILLON	
"	8/7/16	8 am	Sent float to collect two horses at VIGNACOURT	
"	9/7/16	10 am	Collected by float one horse from 21 Sigs at CAVILLON	
"		2 pm	Went to VIGNACOURT to arrange with R.T.O. re boxing of horses. Collected two horses at PICQUIGNY & one at VIGNACOURT. Left N.C.O. & 2 men to complete boxing of animals at 10 am following morning (12 animals)	
	10/7/16	7 am	Left CAVILLON with Hd. Qrs. Chargers & eight section horses for RIBEMONT. The remainder of section with sick horses & Hd Qr. Transport left at 8 am	
		4 pm	arrived RIBEMONT	
	11/7/16	2 pm	Evacuated 28 animals including 5 surf mange & 8 shrapnel wounds. Visited 64 Field ambulance & 21 Div Sigs. Advised improvement in latter horses	
	12/7/16	—	Nothing of note	

33rd Mob. Vety Section

Instructions regarding War Diaries and Intelligence Summaries are contained in F. S. Regs., Part II. and the Staff Manual respectively. Title pages will be prepared in manuscript.

WAR DIARY
or
INTELLIGENCE SUMMARY.

(Erase heading not required.)

Army Form C. 2118.

Place	Date	Hour	Summary of Events and Information	Remarks and references to Appendices
RISGEMONT	13/7/16 ~~13/7/16 10am~~	11am	Pte. Ellen AVC sent to No. 2 Vety Hospital. Surplus to establishment.	
"	14/7/16	2pm	Vacated 24 sick animals (2 mange)	
"		4pm	Visited horses of 64 Field ambulance.	
"	15/7/16		Visited advance section at Mon. de VIVIER. A great many cavalry horses are being sent here. I think the M.V. Secs. of Cavalry Cdn are too far behind.	
"	16/7/16	12am	Vacated 24 sick animals	
		9pm	Mallined (Palpebral Test) three 95 Bde R.F.A. horses	
	17/7/16	3pm	No. 5 M.V. Section arrived. I made arrangements that they should come into my billet for 48 hrs. Reaction to horses tested previous night – Negative	
	18/7/16	2pm	Vacated 43 sick animals, 38 of which were Indian cavalry horses, majority being shrapnel wounds. A great many Indian cavalry horses show slight abrasions on side possibly due to sharp edge of steel below the carried on saddle	
	19/7/16	—	Nothing of note	
"	20/7/16	9am	Vacated 22 sick animals. Mostly shrapnel cases	
		10.30am	Left for Caillon arriving there after good journey 8.30 pm. The axle of ambulance broke mid-way but managed to finish journey. The wood work of RSPCA gift ambulances is not seasoned enough. It never	

T2134. Wt. W708–776. 500000. 4/15. Sir J. C. & S.

33 Mob Vety. Section

WAR DIARY
or
INTELLIGENCE SUMMARY.
(Erase heading not required.)

Army Form C. 2118.

Instructions regarding War Diaries and Intelligence Summaries are contained in F. S. Regs., Part II. and the Staff Manual respectively. Title pages will be prepared in manuscript.

Place	Date	Hour	Summary of Events and Information	Remarks and references to Appendices
	Continued			
Ribemont	20/7/16		Being splinting of wood work of wheels in any place which is bearing extra weight.	
CAVILLON	21/7/16		Nothing of note	
"	22/7/16	1 pm	Collected Two horses at PICQUIGNY for Maire	
"	23/7/16	8 am	Left BOIS de CAVILLON arriving Le CAUROY 9 P.M. [illegible] very good stage watering for animals difficult	
Le CAUROY	24/7/16	10 am	A.D.V.S. inspected section expressed satisfaction	
"	25/7/16	6 am	Sent float to MONCHEAUX to fetch Div Train horse left behind.	
"	26/7/16	10 am	visited horses Auxiliary Horse Transport 3rd Army sent two to M.V. Sec from surp. mange	
		11.30	visited Sub Remount Depot 3rd Army sent them to M.V. Section	
"	27.7.16	11 am	Vacated 12 animals from FREVENT to ABBEVILLE	
"	28.7.16	10 am	Collected one horse from AUBROMETZ at MAIRE · Two others at CONCHY-SUR-CANCHE.	
"	29.7.16	11 am	Vacated 3 sick animals to ABBEVILLE from FREVENT. [illegible] mange	
	30.7.16	10.30	Left Le CAUROY for HABARCQ arriving at 1.45 p.m	
	31.7.16	9 am	visited VI Corps Cavalry. The Veterinary arrangements in this unit are excellent. Horses are in excellent condition & collectively are the best I have seen in [illegible] expeditionary force	[illegible] Capt. O.C. 33 Mob. Vety. Sec.

T2134. Wt. W708—776. 500000. 4/15. Sir J. C. & S.

VOL 12

33 Mobile Vety Section

Instructions regarding War Diaries and Intelligence Summaries are contained in F. S. Regs., Part II. and the Staff Manual respectively. Title pages will be prepared in manuscript.

WAR DIARY
or
INTELLIGENCE SUMMARY.
(Erase heading not required.)

Army Form C. 2118.

Place	Date	Hour	Summary of Events and Information	Remarks and references to Appendices
HABARCQ	1·8·16	10 am	visited Div H.Q. horses, all found in good Condition.	
		3 pm	rifle Inspection of Section	
"	2·8·16	9·30 am	inspected 21 Div Signals, all found in good physical Condition	
		2 pm	Inspected Gas-helmets of section	
"	3·8·16	10 am	Driver Smith A.S.C. attached put under open arrest, was found sleeping while on Guard. he admitted offence. Driver Smith was found guilty, was given 28 days No 2 Field Punishment.	
"	4·8·16	11 am	vacated 17 Sick Animals including 1 Mange.	
"	5·8·16	10 am	Inspected Section rifles & Gas-helmets.	
"	6·8·16	10·30 am	vacated 45 Sick Animals	
"	7·8·16	11 am	Inspected H.Q. 21 Div Horses, all well & fit.	
	8·8·16	12·30 pm	took advance Section to Duisans. found good place for horses & men.	
	9·8·16	9 am	Sent Interpreter kit to French mission.	
		2·30 pm	visited 63 Field Ambulance.	

T2134. Wt. W708—776. 500000. 4/15. Sir J. C. & S.

33 Mobile Vety Section

Instructions regarding War Diaries and Intelligence Summaries are contained in F. S. Regs., Part II. and the Staff Manual respectively. Title pages will be prepared in manuscript.

WAR DIARY
or
INTELLIGENCE SUMMARY.
(*Erase heading not required.*)

Army Form C. 2118.

Place	Date	Hour	Summary of Events and Information	Remarks and references to Appendices
HABARCQ	10·8·16	10.30am	vacated 40 Sick Animals.	
"	11·8·16	10.30am	vacated 18 Sick Animals including 2 Susp Mange	
		2.30am	visited advance Section, very quiet.	
"	12·8·16	11.am	payed men of Section.	
		3.pm	visited 97 Bde R.F.A.	
	13·8·16	10.30am	vacated 31 Sick Animals.	
		2.pm	one Horse died V Rvulus	
		8.pm	Destroyed one horse. Disease Fracture Radius.	
"	14·8·16	9.am	went to look for new billets, having received orders to get ready for moving.	
		3.30pm	Inspectia advance Section	
"	15·8·16	3.pm	A.D.V.S visited Section, very pleased with the work done.	
		4.pm	got ready for moving tomorrow.	
"	16·8·16	8.pm	vacated 18 Sick Animals including 2 Susp Mange.	
		12.pm	left HABARCQ.	
AGNES-les-DUISANS		4.15pm	arrived at new billets, in field, drains well after rain.	
		4.30pm	put Horse lines up, & made Cook House & forage place	

T2134. Wt. W708–776. 500000. 4/15. Sir J. C. & S.

33 Mobile Vety Section

Instructions regarding War Diaries and Intelligence Summaries are contained in F. S. Regs., Part II. and the Staff Manual respectively. Title pages will be prepared in manuscript.

WAR DIARY
or
INTELLIGENCE SUMMARY.
(Erase heading not required.)

Army Form C. 2118.

Place	Date	Hour	Summary of Events and Information	Remarks and references to Appendices
AGNES-les-DUISANS	17·8·16	9. am	made arrangements for horse standings	
"	18·8·16	9.30 am	vacated 16 Sick Animals. going on with Standings for Horses.	
"	19·8·16	10.30 am	D.D.V.S. and A.D.V.S. Inspected Section. D.D.V.S. greatly pleased with arrangements of Section.	
"	20·8·16	10. am	Inspected H.Q. 21 Div Horses. all in good Condition.	
"	21·8·16	11.30 am	having received orders left Section, to take over G.H.Q. 2nd Echelon horses	
		2. pm	Sent wagons to fetch chalk, 2 loads for horse Standings.	
"	22·8·16	11. am	A.D.V.S. Inspected Section	
"	23·8·16	11.30 pm	Capt F. R. Roche Kelly arrived, and took over Commande of Section	
"	24·8·16	9.30 pm	vacated 11 Sick Animals, including 3 Susp Mange.	
"	25·8·16	9.30 pm	vacated 8 Sick Animals	
		2.30 pm	went to R.E. about roofing for Stabling	
	26·8·16	9.30 am	vacated 8 Sick Animals	
	27·8·16	10 am	Inspected 21 Div Signals horses, all in good Condition	
		3. pm	Sent Wagons out to fetch lagging for Edging of Stabling.	
		8. pm	Destroyed 1 Mule, Disease Wd Punct Hock.	
	28·8·16	12. pm	Capt F. R. Roche Kelly had orders to leave Section, to go to Egypt.	

T2134. Wt. W708—776. 500000. 4/15. Sir J. C. & S.

33 Mobile Vety Section

Instructions regarding War Diaries and Intelligence Summaries are contained in F. S. Regs., Part II. and the Staff Manual respectively. Title pages will be prepared in manuscript.

WAR DIARY
or
INTELLIGENCE SUMMARY.
(Erase heading not required.)

Army Form C. 2118.

Place	Date	Hour	Summary of Events and Information	Remarks and references to Appendices
AGNES-LES-DUISANS	29.8.16	5. p m	Capt T. W. W. Wright arrived and took over Command of Section.	
"	30.8.16	9.30 am	vacated 20 Sick Animals including 4 Susp Mange.	
		2. p m	went around Section and found everything in good order.	
"	31.8.16	10 am	Inspected 21 Signals Horses, found them in good Condition	
		11. am	Sent Capt F. Hogg two Chargers to G. H. Q. for him	
		2.30 pm	Inspected Rifles & Gas-helmets of Section	

TWWright. Capt A. V. C
O. C 33 Mobile Vety Section

33 Mobile Vety Section

Instructions regarding War Diaries and Intelligence Summaries are contained in F. S. Regs., Part II. and the Staff Manual respectively. Title pages will be prepared in manuscript.

WAR DIARY
or
INTELLIGENCE SUMMARY.
(Erase heading not required.)

Army Form C. 2118.

Vol 13

Place	Date	Hour	Summary of Events and Information	Remarks and references to Appendices
LE-CAUROY	10·9·16		quiet day	
	11 "	3 pm	Started packing	
	12 "		waitting orders to move	
	13 "	8·45 am	left LE-CAUROY.	
BUIRE	1	4·30 pm	arrived at BUIRE	
	14 "		quiet day.	
	15 "	11 am	Started packing	
	16 "		waitting orders to move	
	17 "	10 am	left BUIRE	
FRICOURT	17 "	2·30 pm	arrived FRICOURT	
	18 "	2 pm	went to Mametz to find place for advance Sections	
	19 "	10 am	took advance Section to Mametz.	
		2·30 pm	A.D.V.S visited Section	
	20 "	8 am	Evacuated 11 Sick Animals	
		2 pm	went to advance Section.	
	21 "	8 am	evacuated 8 Sick Animals.	

T2134. Wt. W708—776. 500000. 4/15. Sir J. C. & S.

33 Mobile Vety Section.

Army Form C. 2118.

Instructions regarding War Diaries and Intelligence Summaries are contained in F. S. Regs., Part II. and the Staff Manual respectively. Title pages will be prepared in manuscript.

WAR DIARY
or
INTELLIGENCE SUMMARY.
(Erase heading not required.)

Place	Date	Hour	Summary of Events and Information	Remarks and references to Appendices
AGNEZ-LES-DUISONS	1.9.16	9.30	Evacuated 16 Sick Animals.	
"	"	2.15	A.D.V.S. visited Section.	
"	2.9.16	9.30	Evacuated 32 Sick Animals including 8 Suspected Mange	
	3.9.16	11. am	Went with A.D.V.S to find new billets for Section	
		3.p.m	Destroyed one Mule, Disease Tetanus.	
	4.9.16	10. am	Inspected R.E. Coy, Horses, all in good Condition.	
	5.9.16	4.am	Evacuated 57 Sick Animals	
		9.30am	left AGNEZ-LES-DUISONS	
LE-CAUROY	5.9.16	4.pm	arrived LE-CAUROY. Good Stabling for horses.	
	6.9.16		quiet day.	
	7.9.16	10.30am	A.D.V.S. & D.A.Q.M.G visited Section.	
			admitted four horses.	
	8.9.16	9.30am	Sent half of Section to Baths.	
		2.pm	held Kit inspection	
	9.9.16	9.30am	Sent second half of Section to Baths	
		2.pm	Payed men of Section. Sent Pte Love & Pte Hickman to No 13 Vety Hospital	

T2134. Wt. W708–776. 500000. 4/15. Sir J. C. & S.

33 Mobile Vety Section

Instructions regarding War Diaries and Intelligence Summaries are contained in F. S. Regs., Part II. and the Staff Manual respectively. Title pages will be prepared in manuscript.

WAR DIARY
or
INTELLIGENCE SUMMARY.
(Erase heading not required.)

Army Form C. 2118.

Place	Date	Hour	Summary of Events and Information	Remarks and references to Appendices
FRICOURT	22.9.16	8.30 am	Evacuated 16 Sick Animals. A.D.V.S visited Section.	
	23 "	8.30 am	Evacuated 21 Sick Animals	
		2 p.m	payed Men of Section	
	24 "	8.30 am	Evacuated 49 Sick Animals, two horses died with G.S.Wds	
		7 pm	Distroyed 2 horses, Disease G.S.Wds	
	25 "	8.30 am	Evacuated 36 Sick Animals. Distroyed 1 Horse Disease G.S.Wds	
	26 "	8.30 am	Evacuated 23 Sick Animals including 2 Susp Mange	
	27 "	8.30 am	Evacuated 46 Sick Animals	
		2 p.m	visited advance Section, everything in Order.	
	28 "	8.30 am	Evacuated 15 Sick Animals.	
		2.30 pm	inspected 21 Division Signals Horses. found all in good Condition	
	29 "	8.30 am	Evacuated 38 Sick Animals	
		2.30 pm	A.D.V.S. visited Section	
	30 "	8.30 am	Evacuated 21 Sick Animals.	
		2 p.m	inspected 21 Division R.E. Horses. found all in good Condition	

[illegible] Capt AVC
Ot. No 33 Mobile Vety Section

T2134. Wt. W708–776. 500000. 4/15. Sir J. C. & S.

33 Mobile Vety Section

Instructions regarding War Diaries and Intelligence Summaries are contained in F. S. Regs., Part II. and the Staff Manual respectively. Title pages will be prepared in manuscript.

WAR DIARY
or
INTELLIGENCE SUMMARY.
(Erase heading not required.)

Army Form C. 2118.

Vol 14

Place	Date	Hour	Summary of Events and Information	Remarks and references to Appendices
FRICOURT	1.10.16	6. am	Evacuated 76 Sick Animals	
		2. pm	went to advance Section, & made preparation for moving next day.	
	2.10.16	11.30am	left Fricourt. Evacuated 2 Sick Animals on line of March	
RIBEMONT	"	3. pm	arrived Ribemont	
	3 "	6.30am	Evacuated 2 Sick Animals.	
		12. pm	left Ribemont	
St, SAUVEUR		8.30pm	arrived at St, Sauveur. good journey. very wet.	
	4 "	9. pm	left St. Sauveur	
FAMECHON		4. pm	arrived Famechon, all horses well, found good Stabling for horses	
	5 "		quiet day.	
	6 "	10 am	Inspected Divisional H^d Q^rs Horses, all found in good condision.	
	7 "	2. pm	Packed readdy for moving	
	8 "	6. am	left Famechon	
		9. am	arrived Abbeville, very wet, Horse Trucks not readdy, had to wait.	
		12. pm	boxed Horses	
		10.30pm	arrived Chocques, unboxed Horses, watered.	

33 Mobile Vety Section

WAR DIARY
or
INTELLIGENCE SUMMARY.
(Erase heading not required.)

Army Form C. 2118.

Instructions regarding War Diaries and Intelligence Summaries are contained in F. S. Regs., Part II. and the Staff Manual respectively. Title pages will be prepared in manuscript.

Place	Date	Hour	Summary of Events and Information	Remarks and references to Appendices
NŒUX-LES-MINES	20·10·16	9.30am	visited advance Section, everything looking well.	
		2·p·m	men went to Baths.	
	21 "	2·p·m	went with A.D.V.S. to inspect Field Remount Section.	
	22 "		quiet day.	
	23 "	10·am	Staff Sergt Harrison went as witness, Against Cpl Davey, of the R.E. Coy.	
		2.30pm	the advance Section has been withdrawn.	
		4.30pm	Payed men of Section.	
	24 "	7·am	Evacuated 8 Sick Animals.	
		2·p·m	Inspected 33 Royal Fusiliers Horses, found all in good Condision	
	25 "	10·am	Inspected 251 Tunneling Coy R.E. Horses, all fit & in good Condision	
	26 "	10·30am	Went to A.D.V.S. Office.	
		2·p·m	Inspected Section rifles.	
	27 "	7·am	Evacuated 21 Sick Animals	
		5·p·m	Driver Smith A.S.C went Sick.	
	28 "	9.30am	visited 1/2 Hants R.E. Horses, all in good Condision	
		2.45pm	visited Div Signals Horses, found fit & in good Condision	

T2134. Wt. W708–776. 500000. 4/15. Sir J. C. & S.

33 Mobile Vety Section.

Instructions regarding War Diaries and Intelligence Summaries are contained in F. S. Regs., Part II. and the Staff Manual respectively. Title pages will be prepared in manuscript.

WAR DIARY
or
INTELLIGENCE SUMMARY.
(Erase heading not required.)

Army Form C. 2118.

Place	Date	Hour	Summary of Events and Information	Remarks and references to Appendices
NŒUX-LES-MINES	29·10·16	7·am	Evacuated 35 Sick Animals.	
		2·p·m	Inspected 2 section 1 Pontoon Park Horses. found in good Condition.	
	30 "	10am	Pte C S. Parker went Sick. went in Hospital.	
	31 "	12·p·m	Evacuated 56 Sick Animals.	
		2.30pm	went with A.D.V.S. to Fleury to inspect some horses, which had been left by the Artillery, on the line of March. these Horses where found fit to travel.	

[illegible] Capt AVC
O.C. No 33 Mobile Vety Section

T2134. Wt. W708–776. 500000. 4/15. Sir J. C. & S.

33 Mobile Vety Section

Instructions regarding War Diaries and Intelligence Summaries are contained in F. S. Regs., Part II. and the Staff Manual respectively. Title Pages will be prepared in manuscript.

WAR DIARY
or
INTELLIGENCE SUMMARY
(Erase heading not required.)

Army Form C. 2118.

21

Vol 15

Place	Date	Hour	Summary of Events and Information	Remarks and references to Appendices
NOEUX-LES-MINES	1.11.16	9.30 am	Inspected 33 Labour Batt Royal Fusiliers, 1/2 Hants R.E, 251 Tunneling Coy R.E, 2 Sect 1 Pontoon Park, 4 7 & 8 Sect 1 Pontoon Park, Horses. these were all found to be in good Condition.	
		4. pm	Sergt James went on leave.	
"	2.11.16	9.30 am	Pte Rogers went Sick. admitted into Hospital.	
"	3.11.16	12.30 pm	Evacuated 72 Sick Animals, to Neuf-Chatel.	
		3. pm	A.D.V.S. visited Section	
"	4.11.16	2. pm	Inspected rifles and Gas-helmets	
"	5.11.16	4. pm	Horse died, Disease Pneumonia.	
"	6.11.16	12.30 pm	Evacuated 32 Sick Animals, to Neuf Chatel.	
		5. pm	Payed Men of Section	
"	7.11.16	11 am	A.D.V.S visited Section.	
"	8.11.16	4.30 pm	Capt T.W.W. Wright proceeded on leave, Capt Turner assumed duty temporarily.	
		2. pm	Collected Head collars 135, from remounts.	
"	9.11.16	9. am	Float Sent to Sailly-Labourse to fetch horse of Capt Turner.	
		2. pm	Went with A.D.V.S. to Auchel to inspect Mule, left behind by the 61 Division	
"	10.11.16	1. pm	Evacuated 14 Sick Animals, including 4 Surp Mange.	
"	11.11.16	2.30 pm	A.D.V.S. visited Section.	
"	12.11.16	12. pm	Evacuated 40 Sick Animals	
"	13.11.16	1. pm	Evacuated 8 Sick Animals	
"	14.11.16		Nothing of note.	

2449 Wt. W14957/M90 750,000 1/16 J.B.C. & A. Forms/C.2118/12.

33 Mobile Vety Section

Instructions regarding War Diaries and Intelligence Summaries are contained in F. S. Regs., Part II. and the Staff Manual respectively. Title Pages will be prepared in manuscript.

WAR DIARY
or
INTELLIGENCE SUMMARY
(Erase heading not required.)

Army Form C. 2118.

Place	Date	Hour	Summary of Events and Information	Remarks and references to Appendices
NOEUX-LES-MINES	15.11.16	10 am	visited 21 Divisional Signals Horses, all in good condition.	
			Pte Brown proceeded on leave.	
"	16.11.16	11 am	Evacuated 10 Sick Animals.	
		2.30 pm	A.D.V.S. visited Section	
"	17.11.16		Corporal Cross and Corporal Farmer were promoted Sergeants from the 30.10.16	
"	18.11.16		nothing of note.	
"	19.11.16		Capt J.W.W. Wright returned from leave.	
"	20.11.16	2 pm	Payed Men of Section.	
"	21.11.16	2.30 pm	inspected rifles of Section.	
"	22.11.16	1 pm	Evacuated 21 Sick Animals including 5 Susp Mange Cases.	
		2.30 pm	half the Men of Section were tested with gas with the new box respirators.	
			L/Cpl Sargett proceed on leave.	
"	23.11.16		Capt J.W.W. Wright assumed duty at A.D.V.S. office, while being away on leave	
		12 pm	Evacuated 11 Sick Animals.	
"	24.11.16	10.30 am	went to A.D.V.S. Office.	
"	25.11.16	9.30 am	Examined scrapings from horse with Susp Mange.	
"	26.11.16	10 am	went with party of men to Bethune, and Collected 140 Head Collars.	
		12 pm	Evacuated 10 Sick Animals.	
"	27.11.16	10 am	visited A.D.V.S. office.	
"	28.11.16		visited 33 Labour Batt, Royal Fusilier horses, all in good Condition	
		2.30 pm	D.D.V.S. visited Section, he was very pleased with Section.	

2449 Wt. W14957/M90 750,000 1/16 J.B.C. & A. Forms/C.2118/12.

33 Mobile Vety Section

Instructions regarding War Diaries and Intelligence Summaries are contained in F. S. Regs., Part II. and the Staff Manual respectively. Title Pages will be prepared in manuscript.

WAR DIARY
or
INTELLIGENCE SUMMARY
(Erase heading not required.)

Army Form C. 2118.

Place	Date	Hour	Summary of Events and Information	Remarks and references to Appendices
NOEUX-LES-MINES	29.11.16	3 p.m	Sergt Cross dispatched to No 12 Veterinary Hospital	
			Sergt Garner dispatched to No 2 Convalescent Horse depot.	
			Dr Holliday proceeded on leave.	
"	30.11.16	9.30 am	Pte Woolley admitted into Hospital.	
		2.30 pm	Men went to baths	
		3 pm	visited A.D.V.S. office.	

J Wolstenholme
Capt A.V.C
O.C 33 Mobile Vety Section

2449 Wt. W14957/M90 750,000 1/16 J.B.C. & A. Forms/C.2118/12.

33 Mobile Veterinary Section

Instructions regarding War Diaries and Intelligence Summaries are contained in F. S. Regs., Part II. and the Staff Manual respectively. Title Pages will be prepared in manuscript.

WAR DIARY
or
INTELLIGENCE SUMMARY
(Erase heading not required.)

Army Form C. 2118.

Vol 16

Place	Date	Hour	Summary of Events and Information	Remarks and references to Appendices
NOEUX-LE-MINES	1.12.16	11.30 am	Evacuated 10 Suspected Mange Cases to Neuf-Chatel.	
		2 pm	Evacuated 13 Sick Animals to St Omer.	
	2.12.16		Collected Head Collars of Remounts.	
	3.12.16	11.30 am	Evacuated 3 Susp Mange Cases at Bethune Station, with No 5 M.V.S.	
			A.D.V.S. returned from leave, & visited section	
		5 pm	Corporal Craig proceeded on leave. Pte Woolley Evacuated to No 4 Station Hospital.	
	4.12.16	2 pm	Payed Men of Section.	
	5.12.16	9.30 am	Inspected 63 Field Ambulance Horses found Suspected Mange among the horses.	
	6.12.16	11 am	A.D.V.S. visited Section.	
		5 pm	Pte Cant proceeded on leave. Evacuated 16 Suspected Mange Cases to Neuf Chatel.	
	7.12.16	8 am	Went with party of N.C.O's and Men to Village of Rely, & collected 4 Sick Animals belonging to 7 Division	
	8.12.16	7.30 pm	arrived back from Rely	
	9.12.16		nothing of note.	
	10.12.16	10.30 am	Evacuated 16 Sick Animals	
		2 pm	visited HQ Qrs Coy 21 Div Train Horses all in good condition	
	11.12.16	9.10 am	visited 63 Field Ambulance horses in good condition.	
		3 pm	Colonel Martin and Mcdonald Major visited Section	
			Pte Goodall sent to Hospital.	
	12.12.16	2 pm	visited 7 & 8 Section 1st Pontoon Park. Horses all looking well.	
	13.12.16	11 am	Evacuated 15 Sick Animals including 8 Susp Mange	
			Pte Hodge proceeded on leave.	
	14.12.16	7 am	Went to Rely with party of N.C.O's and Men to collect horses from 23 Division	
	15.12.16		during day went to villages, to see if any horses were left by 23 division. at Auchy-au-Bois, Westrehem, and Ligny les Aire. after visiting these villages, went on to Burbure and Collected two Horses, left there two months since by 4 Canadian Division, and 3 Division.	

2449 Wt. W14957/M90 750,000 1/16 J.B.C. & A. Forms/C.2118/12.

33 Mobile Veterinary Section

Instructions regarding War Diaries and Intelligence Summaries are contained in F. S. Regs., Part II. and the Staff Manual respectively. Title Pages will be prepared in manuscript.

WAR DIARY
or
INTELLIGENCE SUMMARY

(Erase heading not required.)

Army Form C. 2118.

Place	Date	Hour	Summary of Events and Information	Remarks and references to Appendices
NŒUX-LES-MINES	16.12.16	2 p.m	visited A.D.V.S.	
	17.12.16	10.30 am	Evacuated 16 Sick Animals including 10 Susp Mange.	
		2 p.m	visited 63 Field Ambulance Horses all in good trim.	
	18.12.16	10 am	visited 33 Labour Batt Royal Fusiliers Horses in good condition	
		2 p.m	Payed men of Section.	
	19.12.16	2 p.m	Went to Ordnance Work shop about Float.	
			Sgt Harrison proceeded on leave.	
	20.12.16	9.30 am	Inspection Saddlery belonging to Section	
	21.12.16	11 am	Evacuated 16 Sick Animals.	
		12.30 p.m	Pte Edwards A.V.C. and Pte Thomson A.V.C. reported here for duty	
	22.12.16	2 p.m	Sent party of Men to the Gas School to be tested with new box respirators.	
	23.12.16	11 am	Evacuated 6 Susp Mange Cases to Neuf Chatel	
		2 p.m	Inspected kit, Saddlery & rifles of Section.	
	24.12.16	2 p.m	Went to A.D.V.S. office.	
	25.12.16		nothing of note.	
	26.12.16	11 am	Evacuated 9 Sick Animals to St Omer	
	27.12.16	9 am	visited 33 Labour Batt, Royal Fusiliers and 21 Div Train. Horses all looking well	
			Pte Rees proceeded on leave.	
	28.12.16		nothing of note	
	29.12.16		sent party of N.C.O's and Men to Ligny-les-Aire to collect Horse having been left there by 23rd Division	
	30.12.16		arrived Back from Ligny-les-Aire	
		?.30	Evacuated 16 Sick Animals to Neuf-Chatel.	
	31.12.16	10 am	Went to Bethune to arrange about new billet.	

[signature]
Capt A.V.C.
O.C 33 Mobile Vety Section

33rd Mobile Veterinary Section

Instructions regarding War Diaries and Intelligence Summaries are contained in F. S. Regs., Part II. and the Staff Manual respectively. Title Pages will be prepared in manuscript.

WAR DIARY
or
INTELLIGENCE SUMMARY
(Erase heading not required.)

Army Form C. 2118.

January 1917

Vol 17

Place	Date	Hour	Summary of Events and Information	Remarks and references to Appendices
Noeux les Mines	1st.		nothing to report.	
	2nd		Evacuated 23 sick animals including 7 suspected mange	
	3rd.		nothing to report	
	4th	10am	left Noeux les Mines for Bethune	
Bethune	5th		Evacuated 14 sick animals to St Omer	
	6th		Established an advanced Collecting Station at Ancel – one sergeant & two men who were attached to No 3 Coy 21st Divisional Train for rations. No SE 14896 S.S. McCree of AVC reported for duty	
	7th		~~nothing to report~~ No SE 7192 S.S. French of the AVC transferred to School of Farriery Abbeville	
	8th		nothing to report	
	9th		Evacuated 22 sick animals including 3 suspected mange	
	10th		nothing to report.	
	11th		nothing to report	
	12th		Evacuated 10 sick animals to base	
	13th		nothing to report	
	14th		nothing to report	
	15th		nothing to report	

2449 Wt. W14957/M90 750,000 1/16 J.B.C. & A. Forms/C.2118/12.

33 Mobile Vety Section

Instructions regarding War Diaries and Intelligence Summaries are contained in F. S. Regs., Part II. and the Staff Manual respectively. Title pages will be prepared in manuscript.

WAR DIARY
or
INTELLIGENCE SUMMARY.
(*Erase heading not required.*)

Army Form C. 2118.

Place	Date	Hour	Summary of Events and Information	Remarks and references to Appendices
	8.10.16	2.30am	arrived early hours of morning, NOEUX-LES-MINES.	
NOEUX-LES-MINES	9.10.16		quiet day	
	10"	10 am	A.D.V.S. visited Section, found horses fit + well	
		2.30pm	payed men of Section.	
	11"	10.30am	Pte Hellens got arms burnt. sent to Hospital.	
	12"	9.30am	Went to C.R.E. to find out about Timber for Stables	
	13"	9.am	Went to Bethune, + found out the hours for, Evacuating Sick Animals by barge	
		2.pm	Inspected Sections rifles + Gas helmets.	
	14"	7.am	Evacuated 5 Sick Animals by barge	
		2.30pm	inspected Div Signals Horses, all looking well + fit.	
	15"	2.pm	Inspected Divisional Hd Qrs Horses, all in good Condition	
	16"	11.am	Sent advance Section to Bethune	
	17"	7.am	Evacuated 30 Sick Animals.	
	18"	7.30am	Pte Johnson went on leave	
		2.30pm	visited advance Section	
	19"	7 am	Evacuated 13 Sick Animals. A.D.V.S. visited Section	

T2134. Wt. W708–776. 500000. 4/15. Sir J. C. & S.

Army Form C. 2118.

WAR DIARY
or
INTELLIGENCE SUMMARY
(Erase heading not required.)

33rd Mobile Veterinary Section

Instructions regarding War Diaries and Intelligence Summaries are contained in F. S. Regs., Part II. and the Staff Manual respectively. Title Pages will be prepared in manuscript.

January 1917

Place	Date	Hour	Summary of Events and Information	Remarks and references to Appendices
Bethune	16th		Evacuated 12 sick animals including 5 suspected mange	
	17th		nothing to report.	
	18th		nothing to report	
	19th		nothing to report	
	20th		nothing to report	
	21st		Evacuated 20 sick animals including one case for vice	
	22nd		nothing to report	
	23rd		nothing to report	
	24th		went to Anchy-au-Bois & collected a sick horse left with an inhabitant.	
	25th		nothing to report.	
	26th		Evacuated 23 sick animals + 37 mange cases	
	27th		left Bethune 9 am arrived Hazebrouck 3 30 pm	
Hazebrouck	28th		left Hazebrouck 9 am arrived Herzeele 3 pm	
Herzeele	29th		nothing to report	
	30th		nothing to report	
	31st		left Herzeele village and moved the section into a farm, map reference D 20 B 2.6	

2449 Wt. W14957/M90 750,000 1/16 J.B.C. & A. Forms/C.2118/12.

O.C. No 33 Mob. Vet. Sect [signature] Capt. A.V.C.

Army Form C. 2118.

Instructions regarding War Diaries and Intelligence Summaries are contained in F. S. Regs., Part II. and the Staff Manual respectively. Title Pages will be prepared in manuscript.

33rd Mobile Veterinary Section

WAR DIARY
or
INTELLIGENCE SUMMARY

(Erase heading not required.)

of February 1917

33rd Mob. Vet. Sec.

Vol 18

Place	Date	Hour	Summary of Events and Information	Remarks and references to Appendices
HERZEELE	1st		nothing to report	
	2nd		nothing to report	
	3rd		nothing to report	
	4th		nothing to report	
	5th		nothing to report	
	6th		nothing to report	
	7th		nothing to report	
	8th		nothing to report	
	9th		nothing to report	
	10th		nothing to report	
	11th		nothing to report	
	12th		Evacuated 29 sick animals by road to Veterinary Hospital St Omer. Left Herzeele 9 am arrived Hazebroucke 3 pm.	
HAZEBROUCKE	13th		Left Hazebroucke 7 am arrived Bethune 2 pm.	
BETHUNE	14th		nothing to report	
	15		Left Bethune 10.30 am. arrived Noeux-les-Mines 11.30 am.	
NOEUX-les-MINES	16th		nothing to report	
	17th		nothing to report	
	18th		nothing to report	
	19th		nothing to report	
	20th		Evacuated 48 sick animals including 40 Mange Cases to No 13 Veterinary Hospital Neufchatel	

2449 Wt. W14957/M90 750,000 1/16 J.B.C. & A. Forms/C.2118/12.

33rd Mobile Veterinary Section

Instructions regarding War Diaries and Intelligence Summaries are contained in F. S. Regs., Part II. and the Staff Manual respectively. Title Pages will be prepared in manuscript.

WAR DIARY
or
INTELLIGENCE SUMMARY
(Erase heading not required.)

Army Form C. 2118.

February 1917.

Place	Date	Hour	Summary of Events and Information	Remarks and references to Appendices
NOEUX-LES-MINES	21st		nothing to report.	
	22nd		nothing to report.	
	23rd		nothing to report.	
	24th		nothing to report.	
	25th		nothing to report.	
	26th		nothing to report.	
	27th		Evacuated 58 sick animals including 21 Mange Cases to No 23 Veterinary Hospital, St Omer.	
	28th		nothing to report.	

J Woolnough Capt AVC.
O.C. 33 Mob Vet Section.

2449 Wt. W14957/M90 750,000 1/16 J.B.C. & A. Forms/C.2118/12.

33rd Mobile Veterinary Section

Army Form C. 2118.

WAR DIARY
or
INTELLIGENCE SUMMARY
(Erase heading not required.)

33rd Mobile Veterinary Section

Vol 19

Instructions regarding War Diaries and Intelligence Summaries are contained in F. S. Regs., Part II. and the Staff Manual respectively. Title Pages will be prepared in manuscript.

March 1917.

Place	Date	Hour	Summary of Events and Information	Remarks and references to Appendices
NOEUX les MINES.	1st		Nothing to report.	
	2nd		Evacuated 31 sick animals including four Mange and two Cellulitis. No 3596 Pt Parker A.V.C. proceeded to England on duty.	
	3rd		Nothing to note.	
BETHUNE	4th		Left NOEUX les MINES 10 am arrived BETHUNE 11 30 am.	
	5th		nothing to report.	
	6th		Evacuated 40 Sick animals including 16 Mange + 6 Cellulitis to St OMER	
	7th		nothing to report.	
	8th		nothing to report	
	9th		nothing to report.	
	10th		nothing to report	
HEUCHIN.	11th		Left BETHUNE 9 am arrived HEUCHIN 4 30 pm	
	12th		Nothing to note.	
AUBROMETZ	13th		Left HEUCHIN 10 am arrived AUBROMETZ 5 pm	
BONNIERES	14th		Left AUBROMETZ 8 30 am arrived in BONNIERES 2 pm	
DOULLENS	15th		Left BONNIERES 8 am arrived in DOULLENS 4 pm	
	16th		nothing to report.	
	17th		Evacuated Sixteen Sick animals No SE 7454 PTE WOOLLEY reported for duty.	
	18th		nothing to report.	
	19th		nothing to report	
	20th		nothing to report	

2449 Wt. W14957/M90 750,000 1/16 J.B.C. & A. Forms/C.2118/12.

33rd Mobile Veterinary Section

WAR DIARY
or
INTELLIGENCE SUMMARY

(Erase heading not required.)

Army Form C. 2118.

Instructions regarding War Diaries and Intelligence Summaries are contained in F. S. Regs., Part II. and the Staff Manual respectively. Title Pages will be prepared in manuscript.

March 1917.

Place	Date	Hour	Summary of Events and Information	Remarks and references to Appendices
DOULLENS	21st		nothing to report.	
	22nd		~~nothing to report~~ No 35421 Lce Cpl ALLEN. NF & No 5621 Pte BROOKES NF reported for duty as Skinners	
	23rd		nothing to report.	
	24th		Evacuated 30 sick animals from BOUQUEMAISON including 8 mange cases.	
	25th		nothing to report.	
	26th		nothing to report.	
	27th		nothing to report.	
	28th		Evacuated thirty sick animals including two mange cases to ABBEVILLE also six horse skins	
	29th		Evacuated 3 horse hides to ABBEVILLE	
	30th		Left DOULLENS 10 AM arrived GOUY-EN-ARTOIS 4 30 pm.	
	31st		nothing to report	

J Wolstringham Capt AVC

OC 33rd Mobile Veterinary Section

2449 Wt. W14957/M90 750,000 1/16 J.B.C. & A. Forms/C.2118/12.

33rd Mobile Veterinary Section

Army Form C. 2118.

Instructions regarding War Diaries and Intelligence Summaries are contained in F. S. Regs., Part II. and the Staff Manual respectively. Title Pages will be prepared in manuscript.

WAR DIARY
or
INTELLIGENCE SUMMARY
(Erase heading not required.)

33rd Mob Vet Section

April 1917

Vol 20

Place	Date	Hour	Summary of Events and Information	Remarks and references to Appendices
Gouy-EN-ARTOIS.	1st		nothing to report.	
	2nd.		Evacuated 14 sick animals and six horse skins to Abbeville. Left Gouy-en-Artois 9 am, arrived in a field just outside BAILLEULMONT 10 am	
BAILLEULMONT.	3rd		nothing to report.	
	4th		Left Bailleulmont 8.30 am arrived ADINFER 11 am	
ADINFER	5th		nothing to report.	
	6th		nothing to report	
	7th		Evacuated 56 sick animals including 2 mange cases, also 36 horse hides to Abbeville	
	8th		nothing to report:	
	9th		Established an advanced Collecting Station at BOISLEUX-au-MONT	
	10th		nothing to report.	
	11th		nothing to report:	
	12th		nothing to report.	
	13th		nothing to report.	
	14th		nothing to report	
	15th		nothing to report	
	16th		nothing to report	
	17th		Evacuated 102 sick horses to Abbeville also 78 horse hides	
	18th		nothing to report:	
	19th		nothing to report	

33rd Mobile Veterinary Section

Instructions regarding War Diaries and Intelligence Summaries are contained in F. S. Regs., Part II. and the Staff Manual respectively. Title Pages will be prepared in manuscript.

WAR DIARY
or
INTELLIGENCE SUMMARY
(Erase heading not required.)

Army Form C. 2118.

April 1917

Place	Date	Hour	Summary of Events and Information	Remarks and references to Appendices
ADINFER	20th		Evacuated 9 sick Animals to Abbeville also 79 horse hides.	
	21st		Nothing to report	
	22nd		nothing to report	
	23rd		nothing to report.	
	24th		Evacuated 30 sick Animals to Abbeville also 11 horse hides. Recalled advanced Collecting Station at Boisleux-au-Mont.	
	25th		nothing to report.	
	26th		Left ADINFER 10 am arrived BOISLEUX-au-Mont 11 am	
BOISLEUX-au-MONT.	27th		Evacuated 28 sick Animals including 3 Cellulitis Cases to Abbeville also 4 horse hides.	
	28th		nothing to report	
	29th		nothing to report	
	30th		No1004 Sgt Hill AVC arrived with a party of 10 men from No 22 Veterinary Hospital ABBEVILLE to be attached to the Section	

J Wohlwright. Capt. AVC
O.C. 33rd Mob. Vet. Sec.

2449 Wt. W14957/M90 750,000 1/16 J.B.C. & A. Forms/C.2118/12.

33rd Mobile Veterinary Sect. WAR DIARY

Army Form C. 2118.

Instructions regarding War Diaries and Intelligence Summaries are contained in F. S. Regs., Part II. and the Staff Manual respectively. Title pages will be prepared in manuscript.

May 1917.

or

INTELLIGENCE SUMMARY.

(Erase heading not required.)

Place	Date	Hour	Summary of Events and Information	Remarks and references to Appendices
ADINFER	17th		Nothing to report	
	18th		" "	
	19th		Evacuated to base hospital 15 horses & one mule also sixteen hides	
	20		Nothing to report.	
	21st		" " "	
	22nd		" " "	
	23rd		" "	
	24th		" "	
	25th		"	
	26th		Evacuated to base hospital thirteen horses and one mule also two hides.	
	27th		Nothing to report	
	28th		" " "	
	29th			
	30th		Evacuated to base hospital Eleven horses and two mules also two hides.	
	31st		Left ADINFER 10.30 am arrived BOISLEUX au Mont 12-15 am	

[illegible] Capt AVC OC 33rd Mob Vet Sect.

T2134. Wt. W708-776. 500000. 4/15. Sir J. C. & S.

33rd Mobile Vet: Section

Instructions regarding War Diaries and Intelligence Summaries are contained in F. S. Regs., Part II. and the Staff Manual respectively. Title pages will be prepared in manuscript.

June 1917

WAR DIARY
or
INTELLIGENCE SUMMARY.

(Erase heading not required.)

Army Form C. 2118.

33rd Mobile Veterinary Section

Vol 22

Place	Date	Hour	Summary of Events and Information	Remarks and references to Appendices
Bouzleux.	1st		Nothing to report.	
	2nd		Evacuated 32 horses & 1 mule to Base Hospital. The Medical Officer the Ammunition Train commenced	
			re-inoculation of men of section	
	3rd		Nothing to report	
	4th		Evacuated 21 horses & 2 mules to Base Hospital	
	5th		Nothing to report.	
	6th		Evacuated 4 horses & 1 mule to Base Hospital	
	7th		La Cpl Allen. Pte Brooker & Pte Knott who had been temporarily attached from the Infantry for horse	
			Skinning were returned to their unit.	
	8th		Nothing to report	
	9th		Evacuated 39 horses & 1 mule to hospital by rail also despatched 10 hides.	
	10th		Nothing to report	
	11th		Evacuated 13 horses & 1 mule to Base hospital by rail	
	12th		The DDVS visited Section	
	13th		Evacuated 19 horses to No 7 Vety Hospital	
	14th		Nothing to report	

T2134. Wt. W708–776. 500000. 4/15. Sir J. C. & S.

33rd Mobile Veterinary Section

WAR DIARY
or
INTELLIGENCE SUMMARY.
(Erase heading not required.)

Army Form C. 2118.

Instructions regarding War Diaries and Intelligence Summaries are contained in F. S. Regs., Part II. and the Staff Manual respectively. Title pages will be prepared in manuscript.

June 1917

Place	Date	Hour	Summary of Events and Information	Remarks and references to Appendices
BOISLEUX	15th		Nothing to report	
	16th		Evacuated 13 horses & one mule to Base Vety Hospital by rail	
	17th		Nothing to report	
	18th		Evacuated 38 horses, two mules & one hide to Base by rail	
	19th		Nothing to report	
	20th		Left BOISLEUX 7 am arrived ADINFER 8.30 am Evacuated 9 horses & 2 mules to Base by rail	
ADINFER	21st		Nothing to report	
	22nd		Nothing to report	
	23rd		~~Nothing to report~~ Evacuated 7 horses & 2 mules to Base Hospital by rail	
	24th		Nothing to report	
	25th		Nothing to report	
	26th		Nothing to report	
	27th		Nothing to report	
	28th		Nothing to report	
	29th		Nothing to report	
	30th		Evacuated 19 animals to Base Hospital by rail	

[illegible] Capt. AVC
O.C. 33rd M.V.S

T2134. Wt. W708—776. 500000. 4/15. Sir J. C. & S.

33rd Mobile Veterinary Section.

July 1917.

Army Form C. 2118.

WAR DIARY
or
INTELLIGENCE SUMMARY
(Erase heading not required.)

Instructions regarding War Diaries and Intelligence Summaries are contained in F. S. Regs., Part II. and the Staff Manual respectively. Title Pages will be prepared in manuscript.

Vol 23

Place	Date	Hour	Summary of Events and Information	Remarks and references to Appendices
ADINFER	1st.		Left ADINFER 10.35 am. arrived BOISLEUX au MONT 11.40 am. Took over [illegible] from 42nd M.V.S.	
BOISLEUX-au-MONT.	2nd		Evacuated 13 horses to Base Hospital by rail	
"	3rd		Nothing to report.	
"	4th		Obtained two Sawyer Stoves from Ordnance for use in preparing Calcium Sulphide for treatment of mange	
"	5th		Issued 16 gallons of Calcium Sulphide to units	
"	6th		Pte Keightley 8th Leicester attached as Skinner granted 10 days leave. Issued 19 gallons of Calcium Sulphide	
"	7th		Evacuated 33 horses & 3 mules to Base hospital by rail. Issued 44 gallons of Calcium Sulphide	
"	8th		Two Privates detached for duty at VIIth Corps Horse Dipping Bath at MONDICOURT. Issued 55 gallons of Calcium Sulphide to Units.	
"	9th		Issued five gallons of Calcium Sulphide	
"	10th		Cpl Lewis who had been detached for duty with ADVS VIIth Corps returned to Section for duty. Issued 29 gallons of Calcium Sulphide to Units	
"	11th		Evacuated 18 sick horses including 7 Mange Cases to Base by rail. Issued 13 gallons of Calcium Sulphide	
"	12th		SS. 693 Sgt BUTCHER A.V.C. reported for duty with Section. Issued 16 gallons of Calcium Sulphide to Units.	
"	13th		Issued 40 gallons of Calcium Sulphide to Units	
"	14th		Issued 6 gallons of Calcium Sulphide to Units.	
"	15th		Issued 6 gallons of Calcium Sulphide to Units	
"	16th		One Private detached for duty at VIIth Corps Horse Dipping Bath at MONDICOURT making three in all. Issued 2 gallons of Calcium Sulphide to Units.	

2449 Wt. W14957/M90 750,000 1/16 J.B.C. & A. Forms/C.2118/12.

33rd Mobile Veterinary Section

Army Form C. 2118.

Instructions regarding War Diaries and Intelligence Summaries are contained in F. S. Regs., Part II. and the Staff Manual respectively. Title Pages will be prepared in manuscript.

WAR DIARY
or
INTELLIGENCE SUMMARY
(Erase heading not required.)

July 1917.

Place	Date	Hour	Summary of Events and Information	Remarks and references to Appendices
BOISLEUX au MONT	17th		Issued 14 gallons of Calcium Sulphide to Units.	
	18th		Evacuated 34 sick animals to Base Hospital by rail. Issued 8 gallons of Calcium Sulphide to Units.	
"	19th		Nothing to report.	
"	20th		Cpl Lewis AVC granted leave to Paris 21-7-17 to 31-7-17. Issued 12 gallons of Calcium Sulphide to Units.	
"	21st		Issued 3 gallons of Calcium Sulphide to Units.	
"	22nd		Collected two sick horses from COUIN left by 5th Australian Division.	
"	23rd		Nothing to report.	
"	24th		Nothing to report.	
"	25th		32 Sick Animals Evacuated to Base by rail. Issued 42 gallons of Calcium Sulphide to Units.	
"	26th		Sent Horse Float to PAS en ARTOIS to collect sick horse. Issued 18 gallons of Calcium Sulphide to Units.	
"	27th		Issued 21 gallons of Calcium Sulphide to Units.	
"	28th		Evacuated to Base by rail 7 horses + 1 mule also 3 horse hides. Issued 6 gallons of Calcium Sulphide to Units.	
"	29th		Nothing to report.	
"	30th		Evacuated 16 horses to Base Hospital by rail. Issued 19 gallons of Calcium Sulphide to Units.	
"	31st		Sent 1 N.C.O. + two men to take over place for M.V.S. at BOIRY St. ~~[illegible]~~ RICTRUDE and to put up horse lines. Issued 14 gallons of Calcium Sulphide to Units.	

[illegible] Capt AVC.
O.C. 33rd Mob Vet Sect.

2449 Wt. W14957/M90 750,000 1/16 J.B.C. & A. Forms/C.2118/12.

Army Form C. 2118.

WAR DIARY
or
INTELLIGENCE SUMMARY
(Erase heading not required.)

Instructions regarding War Diaries and Intelligence Summaries are contained in F. S. Regs., Part II. and the Staff Manual respectively. Title Pages will be prepared in manuscript.

August 1917

33rd Mobile Vet. Sec.

Vol 24

Place	Date	Hour	Summary of Events and Information	Remarks and references to Appendices
BOISLEUX-au-MONT.	1st		Evacuated to Base Hospital by rail 13 horses, two mules + two hides	
BOIRY St RICTRUDE	2nd		Left BOISLEUX-au-MONT 10 am. Arrived BOIRY St RICTRUDE [illegible]	
"	3rd		nothing to report	
	4th		Evacuated to Base Hospital by rail 19 horses.	
	5th		nothing to report.	
	6th		Issued 26 gallons of Calcium Sulphide to units to be used for treatment of mange	
	7th		nothing to report	
	8th		Evacuated to Base Hospital by rail 21 sick animals also 3 hides.	
	9th		Issued [illegible] gallons of Calcium Sulphide to units.	
	10th		nothing to report	
	11th		Issued 29 gallons of Calcium Sulphide to units	
	12th		nothing to report	
	13th		Evacuated to base hospital 43 sick animals also 2 hides.	
	14th		nothing to report	
	15th		Evacuated to base hospital [illegible] sick animals.	
	16th		nothing to report	
	17th		Issued 34 gallons of Calcium Sulphide to units.	
	18th		nothing to report	
	19th		nothing to report	
	20th		Evacuated to base hospital 48 sick animals and five hides	

33rd Mob. Vet Sect

Army Form C. 2118.

WAR DIARY
or
INTELLIGENCE SUMMARY
(Erase heading not required.)

Instructions regarding War Diaries and Intelligence Summaries are contained in F. S. Regs., Part II. and the Staff Manual respectively. Title Pages will be prepared in manuscript.

AUGUST 1917

Place	Date	Hour	Summary of Events and Information	Remarks and references to Appendices
BOIRY St. RICTRUDE.	21st.		Nothing to report	
	22nd		Evacuated to base hospital 54 sick animals also 1 hide	
	23rd		Admitted a number of six Corps Cavalry horses for evacuation.	
	24th.		Evacuated 173 sick & DOR cases of VI Corps Cavalry from BEAUMETZ Station in charge of 1 officer & 1 man per eight horse.	
	25th.		Evacuated 39 sick animals also 2 hides to Base hospital by rail	
	26th		Nothing to report.	
AGNEZ-les-DUISANS.	27th.		Left BOIRY St. RICTRUDE at 9.30 am. arrived AGNEZ-les-DUISANS 2.30 pm ~~left~~ handed over Section to OC 47th M.V.S. also seven sick animals for evacuation	
	28th.		Nothing to report.	
	29th.		Nothing to report	
	30		Nothing to report	
	31st		Nothing to report	

J. Wolwright Capt AVC
OC 33rd Mob. Vet Sect.

2449 Wt. W14957/M90 750,000 1/16 J.B.C. & A. Forms/C.2118/12.

33rd Mobile Veterinary Section.

WAR DIARY
or
INTELLIGENCE SUMMARY

(Erase heading not required.)

Army Form C. 2118.

Instructions regarding War Diaries and Intelligence Summaries are contained in F. S. Regs., Part II. and the Staff Manual respectively. Title Pages will be prepared in manuscript.

September 1917

Vol 25

Place	Date	Hour	Summary of Events and Information	Remarks and references to Appendices
AGNES-les DUISANS	1st		Evacuated Seven Sick animals to ABBEVILLE from Railhead at Agnez	
	2nd		nothing to report	
	3rd		nothing to report	
	4th		nothing to report	
	5th		Evacuated eleven sick animals to ABBEVILLE by rail	
	6th		nothing to report	
	7th		nothing to report	
	8th		nothing to report	
	9th		nothing to report	
	10th		Evacuated Eight sick animals to ABBEVILLE by rail	
	11th		nothing to report	
	12th		nothing to report	
	13th		Pte NELLINS A.V.C. was admitted to Bethnal Green Hospital whilst on leave	
	14th		nothing to report	
	15th		Evacuated [illegible] sick animals to ABBEVILLE by rail.	
	16th		Section left AGNEZ les DUISANS at 1 pm for AUBIGNY where we Entrained at 3.20 pm. arriving at CASSEL at 11.30 pm, detrained & watered horses, left CASSEL at 12.30 AM arriving at CAESTRE at 4 am, horses arrived in good order, were billeted in a Farm just off the CAESTRE - CASSEL Road 300 yds from the railway crossing at CAESTRE	

2449 Wt. W14957/M90 750,000 1/16 J.B.C. & A. Forms/C.2118/12.

33rd Mobile Veterinary Section.

Army Form C. 2118.

WAR DIARY
or
INTELLIGENCE SUMMARY
(Erase heading not required.)

Instructions regarding War Diaries and Intelligence Summaries are contained in F. S. Regs., Part II. and the Staff Manual respectively. Title Pages will be prepared in manuscript.

SEPTEMBER 1915.

Place	Date	Hour	Summary of Events and Information	Remarks and references to Appendices
CAESTRE	17th		Erected horse lines in an open field near the farm, the men were billeted in a barn	
	18th		No SS. 2517 Pte MORVILLE J. B. AVC reported here for duty.	
	19th		nothing to report	
	20th		One N.C.O. & two men detached for duty with Xth Corps Mob: Vety: Detachment.	
	21st		Evacuated 1 sick animal as hide to Xth Corps Mob. Vety: Detachment	
	22nd		Evacuated 15 sick animals by road to St Omer, these animals marched to No 8 Rear Sick horse Halt at STAPLE, before they start the night, arriving at No 23 Vety Hospital the following day	
	23rd		nothing to report:	
	24th		Left CAESTRE 9.30 am handing over billet to 41st Divisional M.V.S. arrived at METEREN at 11 am and billeted in a farm just outside the village. Erected horse lines in open for horses, the men were billeted in the barn	
METEREN	25th		nothing to report.	
	26th		Evacuated to sick animals unable to walk by motor ambulance to St Omer.	
	27th		Collected two sick animals from CAESTRE left behind by the 41st Division, Evacuated 9 sick animals to Xth Corps M.V.D.	
	28th		nothing to report.	
	29th		Left METEREN 10 am arrived at N7 a 7.2 near La CLYTTE at 2.30 pm & occupied a piece of ground.	
LA CLYTTE.	30th		Drew posts from 98th Field Coy RE & erected horse lines also procured 4 trench shelters from Area Commandant for use of the men.	

2449 Wt. W14957/M90 750,000 1/16 J.B.C. & A. Forms/C.2118/12.

[signature] Capt. A.V.C. O.C. 33rd Mob Vet Sec

33rd Mobile Veterinary Section.

Army Form C. 2118.

WAR DIARY
or
INTELLIGENCE SUMMARY

(Erase heading not required.)

Instructions regarding War Diaries and Intelligence Summaries are contained in F. S. Regs., Part II. and the Staff Manual respectively. Title Pages will be prepared in manuscript.

October 1917.

33rd Mob. Veterinary Section

Vol 26

Place	Date	Hour	Summary of Events and Information	Remarks and references to Appendices
La CLYTTE	1st.		3pm. moved the section into ZEVECOTEN and took over a covered standing evacuated by B Echelon 21st DAC. good standings for 80 horses and billets for the men.	
ZEVECOTEN	2nd.		Admitted a number of bomb wounds.	
"	3rd.		Evacuated 12 sick animals – walking cases – by road to St Omer	
"	4th		nothing to report	
"	5th		Evacuated 40 sick animals from Vety C.C.S BOESCHEPE chiefly bomb wounds also 41 horse hides.	
"	6th		nothing to report.	
"	7th		B echelon 21st D.A.C. returned to occupy billets, the Section was moved across the road into R.A Headquarters billet. Good standings for horses.	
"	8th		Evacuated 28 sick animals through Vety C.C.S to the base also three horse hides.	
"	9th		Left ZEVECOTEN 8 am. marched through HAZEBROUCK and arrived at RACQUINGHAM 5.30 p.m.	
RACQUINGHAM	10th		Billeted in a farm just outside the village, horses in an open field, men in a farm stable	
"	11th		nothing to report.	
"	12th		nothing to report.	
"	13th		Eleven Privates ~~[illegible]~~ AVC reported for duty to replace eleven "Category A" men of Section.	
"	14th		Eleven "Category A" Privates proceeded to No 5 Base Veterinary Hospital. Evacuated nine sick animals by road to St Omer	
"	15th		nothing to report	
"	16th		nothing to report.	

2449 Wt. W14957/M90 750,000 1/16 J.B.C. & A. Forms/C.2118/12.

33rd Mobile Veterinary Section

Instructions regarding War Diaries and Intelligence Summaries are contained in F. S. Regs., Part II. and the Staff Manual respectively. Title Pages will be prepared in manuscript.

WAR DIARY
or
INTELLIGENCE SUMMARY

(Erase heading not required.)

Army Form C. 2118.

October 1917

Place	Date	Hour	Summary of Events and Information	Remarks and references to Appendices
RACQUINGHAM.	17th		Evacuated seven sick animals by road to St. Omer, also 1 hide.	
"	18th		Nothing to report	
"	19th		Evacuated seven sick animals also 1 hide.	
"	20th		Left RACQUINGHAM 8. am. Arrived La Clyte 5.30 pm no billet at present available so put up at an Infantry Camp at RENINGHELST for the night arrived in 9. pm	
RENINGHELST	21st		Left RENINGHELST 2 pm arrived La CLYTE 3 pm. and took over Mobile Section Billet from No 35 M.V.S. also 25 sick horses. Cover for 60 horses + good billet for men.	
LA. CLYTE	22nd		Sent two men to Advanced Vety Aid Post at Shrapnel Corner, with orders to dress wounded horses, these men were given two days rations.	
"	23rd		Evacuated 28 sick animals through Vety C.C.S. X Corps at OUDERDOM.	
"	24th		Evacuated 24 animals - walking cases - by road to St. OMER	
"	25th		Evacuated one float-case to Vety C.C.S Drew 200 Splits for standings from R.E. Dump.	
"	26th		Sent 1 N.C.O + two men to 21st Divisional Clipping Camp for duty.	
"	27th		Evacuated 30 sick animals from OUDERDOM.	
"	28th		Evacuated one sick animal to OUDERDOM. The horse float has been constantly at work since 22nd inst. a large proportion of the sick animals dealt with are bomb wounds a number of which had to be destroyed and are buried in a field adjoining the section.	

2449 Wt. W14957/M90 750,000 1/16 J.B.C. & A. Forms/C.2118/12.

32nd Mobile Veterinary Section.

WAR DIARY
or
INTELLIGENCE SUMMARY
(Erase heading not required.)

Army Form C. 2118.

Instructions regarding War Diaries and Intelligence Summaries are contained in F. S. Regs., Part II. and the Staff Manual respectively. Title Pages will be prepared in manuscript.

October 1917

Place	Date	Hour	Summary of Events and Information	Remarks and references to Appendices
LA CLYTE	29th		A slight case of Stomatitis was discovered among the sick animals admitted and isolated	
"	30th		Nothing to report of note. Horses coming into M.V.S. in large numbers.	
"	31st		Evacuated 63 sick animals – walking cases. Chiefly Debility by road to St. Omer in charge of 12 mounted men of Section.	

[illegible] Lieut. A.V.C.
O.C. 33rd Mob Vet Sect.

33rd Mobile Veterinary Section.

WAR DIARY
or
INTELLIGENCE SUMMARY.
(Erase heading not required.)

Army Form C. 2118.

33rd Mob. Veterinary Section

Vol 27

Instructions regarding War Diaries and Intelligence Summaries are contained in F. S. Regs., Part II. and the Staff Manual respectively. Title pages will be prepared in manuscript.

November 1917.

Place	Date	Hour	Summary of Events and Information	Remarks and references to Appendices
La Clyte	1st		Evacuated 40 sick animals and sixty horse hides to V.CCS at OUDERDOM for the Base.	
"	2nd		Evacuated three sick animals to V.CCS OUDERDOM.	
			Twelve coolies from 75th Labour Group reported for duty to assist in cleaning horse lines and to dig graves for horses destroyed.	
"	3rd		Evacuated 40 sick animals to St Omer by road	
"	4th		nothing to report.	
"	5th		nothing to report.	
"	6th		Evacuated 30 sick animals to Vety CCS OUDERDOM	
"	7th		Evacuated 19 sick animals by road to St Omer	
"	8th		Evacuated 14 sick animals including 6 mange cases to NEUFCHATEL by Train	
"	9th		nothing to report.	
"	10th		Evacuated 40 sick animals by road to St OMER	
"	11th		Sgt. Butcher AVC detailed for duty at X Corps M.V.D. returned to the section.	
"	12th		nothing to report	
"	13th		1st New Zealand MVS arrived to take over the Section & horse lines temporarily to Section vacated by 5th Division M.V.S. as the Section had no orders to move.	
"	14th		Arranged to evacuate all sick before leaving.	
"	15th		Evacuated 68 sick animals & 112 hides to CCS OUDERDOM.	
"	16th		Hand over Section to 1st NZ MVS left La Clyte 9 am arrived DOULIEU 2.30pm. stable for horses & a barn for the men.	

D. D. & L., London, E.C. (A8001) Wt. W1771/M2031 750,000 5/17 Sch. 52 Forms/C2118/14

32nd Mobile Veterinary Section

WAR DIARY
or
INTELLIGENCE SUMMARY.
(Erase heading not required.)

Army Form C. 2118.

Instructions regarding War Diaries and Intelligence Summaries are contained in F. S. Regs., Part II. and the Staff Manual respectively. Title pages will be prepared in manuscript.

November 1917

Place	Date	Hour	Summary of Events and Information	Remarks and references to Appendices
DOULIEU	17th		Moved into another billet at DOULIEU that had been occupied before by a [illegible]	
"	18th		Left DOULIEU 11 am arrived at BELLERIVE 4 pm. Horses in the open, men in a barn	
BELLERIVE	19th		Left BELLERIVE 8 am arrived at HERSIN 2 pm. Good billets for men & horses. At 9.15 pm a shell burst on a dug-out in the Section [illegible] 4 men who were buried in the debris and badly bruised, they were got out [illegible] and were sent to 64th Field Ambulance. Four horses were also wounded [illegible].	
HERSIN	20th		At 8 am a shell burst near the Section and several others [illegible] of about 10 minutes shelled in the vicinity. At 9.30 I moved the Section out to billets [illegible] another [illegible] in Hersin half a mile away. Casualties four horses [illegible]	
	21st		Nothing to report	
	22nd		Left HERSIN 8 am. Arrived at ANZIN at 2 pm [illegible] sick from 47th Divisional M.V.S. [illegible]	
ANZIN	23rd		Nothing to report	
	24th		Admitted a few sick from the Division	
	25th		Nothing to report	
	26th		Nothing to report	
	27th		Nothing to report	

D. D. & L., London, E.C.
(A8001) Wt. W1771/M2031 750,000 5/17 Sch. 52 Forms C2118/14

32nd Mob Vet Sect.

WAR DIARY
or
INTELLIGENCE SUMMARY.
(Erase heading not required.)

Army Form C. 2118.

Instructions regarding War Diaries and Intelligence Summaries are contained in F. S. Regs., Part II. and the Staff Manual respectively. Title pages will be prepared in manuscript.

November 1917.

Place	Date	Hour	Summary of Events and Information	Remarks and references to Appendices
ANZIN	28th		Evacuated 36 animals by rail from ECURIE to Base Hospital at ABBEVILLE.	
	29th		Evacuated two sick animals by motor float to LILLERS for slaughter for food	
	30th		Handed over all sick - 13 - to 31st Divisional M.V.S. at ECURIE.	

[illegible] Capt AVC
OC 32nd Mobile Vety Section.

D. D. & L., London, E.C.
(A8001) Wt. W1771/M2031 750,000 5/17 Sch. 52 Forms/C2118/14

33rd Mobile Veterinary Section

Instructions regarding War Diaries and Intelligence Summaries are contained in F. S. Regs., Part II. and the Staff Manual respectively. Title pages will be prepared in manuscript.

WAR DIARY
or
INTELLIGENCE SUMMARY.

(Erase heading not required.)

December 1917

Army Form C. 2118.

Vol 28

Place	Date	Hour	Summary of Events and Information	Remarks and references to Appendices
ANZIN.	1st.		Left ANZIN 8 am Arrived BEAULENCOURT 4 pm	
BEAULENCOURT.	2nd		Left BEAULENCOURT 8 am arrived BOUCLY 3.30 pm Section animals were given part of a stable occupied by 21st D.A.C.	
BOUCLY	3rd.		Moved Section with standings near TINCOURT, horses covered, men accomodated in huts	
TINCOURT	4th.		Left TINCOURT 10.30 am. arrived VILLERS FAUCON 1 pm. camped [illegible] near the 51st Divisional M.V.S. who allotted a barn for Section horses, men billeted in a cellar.	
VILLERS-FAUCON	5th.		were allotted cover for 20 sick horses by 5th Div. M.V.S. [illegible] has been recently erected with no standings yet put down	
	6th.		Commenced to build standings for sick horses of broken brick, also cook house for men, forage house & Pharmacy	
	7th.		nothing to report.	
	8th.		nothing to report, work on standings continued	
	9th.		nothing to report	
	10th.		nothing to report	
	11th.		Evacuated three sick animals by rail from ROISEL to No 1 Base Vety Hospital	
	12th.		nothing to report.	
	13th.		nothing to report.	

D. D. & L., London, E.C.
(A8001) Wt. W1771/M2031 750,000 5/17 Sch. 52 Forms/C2118/14

32nd Mobile Veterinary Section

Army Form C. 2118.

WAR DIARY
or
INTELLIGENCE SUMMARY.
(Erase heading not required.)

Instructions regarding War Diaries and Intelligence Summaries are contained in F. S. Regs., Part II. and the Staff Manual respectively. Title pages will be prepared in manuscript.

DECEMBER 1917

Place	Date	Hour	Summary of Events and Information	Remarks and references to Appendices
VILLERS FAUCON.	14.		Evacuated Eight Sick Animals to Base Vety Hospital	
	15th		Brick standing for sick horse stable Completed.	
	16th		nothing to report.	
	17th		nothing to report.	
	18th		Evacuated 12 Sick Animals to Base Vety Hospital	
	19th		nothing to report.	
	20th		nothing to report.	
	21st		Evacuated Six sick animals to Base Vety Hospital.	
	22nd		nothing to report.	
	23rd		nothing to report.	
	24th		nothing to report.	
	25th		nothing to report.	
	26th		Pte Crane AVC admitted to 63rd Field Ambulance with burns, contracted owing to an accident whilst acting as clerk to DADVS	
	27th		nothing to report.	
	28th		Evacuated 24 Sick Animals to Base Vety Hospital.	
	29th		nothing to report	
	30th		nothing to report.	
	31st		Pte BOWMAN AVC being unfit for duty in an M.V.S. was sent to No 5 Vety Hospital for duty.	

J Lobbingham Capt AVC O.C. 32nd Mob Vet. Sect.

D. D. & L., London, E.C.
(A8001) Wt. W1771/M2031 750,000 5/17 Sch. 52 Forms/C2118/14

33rd Mobile Veterinary Section.

Instructions regarding War Diaries and Intelligence Summaries are contained in F. S. Regs., Part II. and the Staff Manual respectively. Title pages will be prepared in manuscript.

WAR DIARY
or
INTELLIGENCE SUMMARY.
(Erase heading not required.)

January 1918

Army Form C. 2118.

Vol 29

Place	Date	Hour	Summary of Events and Information	Remarks and references to Appendices
VILLERS FAUCON.	1st		Pte. BAIRSTOW & CULLINGHAM reported to the Section for duty as reinforcements. Evacuated nine sick animals to Base Veterinary Hospital.	
	2nd		nothing to report.	
	3rd		nothing to report.	
	4th		Evacuated 13 sick animals to Base Vety. Hospital	
	5th		nothing to report	
	6th		Nothing to report	
	7th		nothing to report	
	8th		Evacuated 17 sick animals to Base Vety. Hospital	
	9th		nothing to report	
	10th		nothing to report	
	11th		Evacuated three sick animals to Base Vety. Hospital.	
	12th		Left VILLERS FAUCON 9.30 am arrived QUINCONCE 12 Am	
QUINCONCE	13th		Took over M.V.S. site from 1st AUSTRALIAN Division, good standings for horses but no cover, a great deal of manure about, most of it had been there for some time, men billeted in cellars, Office & O.C.s billet in PERONNE	
	14th		received 16 sick for evacuation from 21st M.V.S. also some sick from 21st Div & Corps Troops	
	15th		Evacuated 21 sick animals to Base Vety Hospital from La Chapellette, which is to be our railhead for evacuation in future.	
	16th		Arranged a manure dump near section with Sanitary Officer also Burial Ground for horses began to Cart away manure from section site	
	17th		Began to erect a forage barn, material obtained from C.R.E. 21st Division	
	18th		Evacuated 28 sick animals, 14 for 21st M.V.S.	

33rd Mobile Veterinary Section

WAR DIARY
or
INTELLIGENCE SUMMARY.
(Erase heading not required.)

Army Form C. 2118.

Instructions regarding War Diaries and Intelligence Summaries are contained in F. S. Regs., Part II. and the Staff Manual respectively. Title pages will be prepared in manuscript.

January

Place	Date	Hour	Summary of Events and Information	Remarks and references to Appendices
QUINCONCE	19th		Forage Barn finished, manure carting proceeded with	
	20th		Got a fatigue party of 3 men from Town Major PERONNE to dig graves for two horses destroyed in the Section	
	21st		VII Corps R.E. officer visited Section to report on site for stables	
	22nd		Evacuated 37 sick animals to Base Vety Hospital	
	23rd		MANGE Stable to accommodate 20 cases completed. A quantity of Calcium Sulphide issued to Division & Corps units.	
	24th		Main standing for horses cleared of manure and brick rubble - about 150 loads was removed to the new manure dump since 16th.	
	25th		Evacuated 32 sick animals to Base Vety Hospital 12 were from 21st M.V.S.	
	26th		Erected a small store near forage barn also commenced to build a forge	
	27th		Indented on CRE 21st Division for material to construct saddle room	
	28th		Forge completed & work on saddle room commenced.	
	29th		Evacuated 80 sick animals to Base Vety Hospital 17 from 21st M.V.S.	
	30th		nothing to report	
	31st		nothing to report	

J. Wolwright Capt. AVC
O.C. 33rd Mobile Vety Section.

D. D. & L., London, E.C. (A8001) Wt. W1771/M2031 750,000 5/17 Sch. 52 Forms/C2118/14

33rd Mobile Veterinary Section (21D)

WAR DIARY
or
INTELLIGENCE SUMMARY.
(Erase heading not required.)

Army Form C. 2118.

Instructions regarding War Diaries and Intelligence Summaries are contained in F. S. Regs., Part II. and the Staff Manual respectively. Title pages will be prepared in manuscript.

February 1918

11 Vol 30

Place	Date	Hour	Summary of Events and Information	Remarks and references to Appendices
QUINCONCE	1st		Evacuated Sick Animals to Base Vety Hospital 55 including 17 from 21st M.V.S.	
	2nd		VII Corps R.E.s commenced a stable for sick horses to accommodate 75 animals.	
	3rd		Saddle Room completed	
	4th		nothing to report, stable construction proceeding	
	5th		Evacuated 59 Sick animals to Base Vety Hospital including 12 from 50th M.V.S and 6 from 21st M.V.S	
	6th		Got a fatigue party of 3 men from Town Major Peronne to assist in moving manure	
	7th		Applied to Mission Agricole Francais for a plough.	
	8th		Evacuated 40 Sick Animals to Base Vety Hospital including 20 from 50th M.V.S.	
	9th		Arranged with Mr Fagot of FLAMICOURT to take horses to be sold for food. Sold a L.D. horse to him for 147 frs for that purpose.	
	10th		Pte HARRIS A. TT 02158 reported as a reinforcement bringing the personnel up to full strength	
	11th		VII Corps R.E.s completed stable for sick horses.	
	12th		Evacuated 67 Sick Animals to Base Vety Hospital including 32 from 50th M.V.S	
	13th		Commenced to build a small stable to hold 8. to be used as an isolation stable for Ulcerative Cellulitis	
	14th		~~Commenced~~ to Ploughed about ¼ of an acre of ground near the M.V.S to be used for growing potatoes &c.	
	15th		Evacuated 45 Sick animals to Base Vety Hospital including 25 from 50th M.V.S	
	16th		Cpl Leon granted 4 days special leave to PARIS.	
			Sergt G Butcher proceeded on leave to U.K.	

D. D. & L., London, E.C.
(A8001) Wt. W1771/M2031 750,000 5/17 Sch. 52 Forms/C2118/14

33rd Mobile Vet. Section

WAR DIARY

or

~~INTELLIGENCE SUMMARY.~~

Army Form C. 2118.

Instructions regarding War Diaries and Intelligence Summaries are contained in F. S. Regs., Part II. and the Staff Manual respectively. Title pages will be prepared in manuscript.

February 1918

(Erase heading not required.)

Place	Date	Hour	Summary of Events and Information	Remarks and references to Appendices
GUINCONCE	17th		Nothing to report.	
	18th		" "	
	19th		Capt. Wright left on leave to U.K. and is relieved by Capt. H.D. Sparrow. Evacuated 64 horses and 20 mules. 8 men were given instruction in musketry on a range.	
	20th		Nothing to report.	
	21st		" "	
	22nd		Evacuated sick animals. 33rd M.V.S. = 16 animals – 50th M.V.S. = 17 animals. Another 8 men instructed in musketry.	
	~~23rd~~			
	23rd		Pte Hayes proceeded on leave to U.K. Paid men of Section.	
	24th		Nothing to report.	
	25th		" "	
	26th		Evacuated sick animals 33rd M.V.S. = 19 animals 50th M.V.S. = 19 animals	
	27th		Nothing to report.	
	28th		" "	

H.D. Sparrow
Capt. A.V.C.
for O.C. 33rd Mobile Vet Section.

D. D. & L., London, E.C.
(A8001) Wt. W1771/M2031 750,000 5/17 Sch. 52 Forms/C2118/14

33rd Mobile Vet Section

7

21

Instructions regarding War Diaries and Intelligence Summaries are contained in F. S. Regs., Part II. and the Staff Manual respectively. Title pages will be prepared in manuscript.

WAR DIARY
or
~~INTELLIGENCE SUMMARY.~~
(Erase heading not required.)

March 1918.

Army Form C. 2118.

Vol 30

Place	Date	Hour	Summary of Events and Information	Remarks and references to Appendices
March 1st Le Quinconce	March 1st		Evacuated 37 sick animals:- 19 from 33rd MVS. + 18 from 50th MVS.	
PERONNE	2nd		Nothing to report	
"	3rd		" "	
" "	4			
" "	5th		Evacuated 39 sick animals:- 29 from 33rd MVS. + 10 from 50th MVS.	
" "	6th		Nothing to report	
" "	7		" "	
" "	8th		Evacuated 91 sick animals:- 25 from 33rd MVS. – 28 from 50th MVS – 38 from 47th MVS.	
" "	9th		Paid men of Section. Capt Wright returned from leave.	
" "	10th		Section ceased to act as Vet. Evacuation Station of VII Corps and moved from QUINCONCE at 10 am. arriving at DRIENCOURT at noon. Capt. T W W WRIGHT + Staff Sergt. W HARRISON transferred to proper organised & authorised VII Corps. Vet. Evacuation Station. Five other men left with this unit in command. Capt. H. D. SPARROW officially takes over command of 33rd M. V. S.	
DRIENCOURT	11		Built stables sheds horselines etc.	
" "	12		" " " "	
" "	13		" " " " "	
" "	14		Pte. Mayes reported back from leave was accidentally kicked on back and admitted to 63rd Field Ambulance. Sent 19 sick horses to VII Corps V.E.S. for evacuation.	
" "	15		Pte Pritchard proceeded on leave.	
" "	16		Sgt. Butcher returned from leave for duty having been detained at home on account of measles breaking out in family	

D. D. & L., London, E.C.
(A5001) Wt. W1771/M2031 750,000 5/17 Sch. 52 Forms/C2118/14

33rd Mobile Vet. Section

WAR DIARY
or
~~INTELLIGENCE SUMMARY.~~
(Erase heading not required.)

Army Form C. 2118.

Instructions regarding War Diaries and Intelligence Summaries are contained in F. S. Regs., Part II. and the Staff Manual respectively. Title pages will be prepared in manuscript.

March 1918.

Place	Date	Hour	Summary of Events and Information	Remarks and references to Appendices
DRIENCOURT	MARCH 17		Nothing to report	
" "	18		Pte. HOOKER H. reported for duty as skinner. Evacuated 15 sick animals to VII Corps V.E.S.	
" "	19		Nothing to report	
" "	20		" " "	
" "	21		Pte Morville returned to Section from leave after being detained two days at HAVRE. Corpl. Levie proceeded on leave. Pte Mayes evacuated to England from a base Hospital as a result of the kick in back received on 14th inst. Evacuated 14 sick animals. Section was shelled with H.E. groundbursts. Had to send men + horses to sunken road for shelter for their dinners. No casualties + material damage slight.	
DRIENCOURT + FEUILLAUCOURT	22		Moved from DRIENCOURT at 10-30 A.M. under searching shellfire. No casualties. 1 N.C.O. + 4 men left for collection + evacuation of sick & wounded horses. 20 animals collected + evacuated to VII Corps V.E.S. Men all rejoined M.V.S. at 10 P.M. at FEUILLAUCOURT where we stood to all night.	
CLERY – HEM BRAY-sur-SOMME	23		Section moved off at 5.30 am to CLERY – stood to there from 9 am – 11.45 am. – moved to HEM watered + fed horses + had dinner + moved off again ~~at~~ at 4.30 P.M. to BRAY-sur-SOMME arriving there at 10 p.m. Stood to all ~~day~~ night.	
" " "	24		Evacuated 4 sick horses to VII Corps V.E.S. Moved into another field + stood to all day + night.	
" " " ETINEHEM VAUX sur SOMME	25		Moved from BRAY sur SOMME at 9.30 AM. Arrived at ETINEHEM at 11.15 am. Corpl. Levie reported back for duty after having his leave cancelled. Stood to all day + moved again at 10.30 pm to VAUX-sur-SOMME arriving at 2.30 am.	
" " BAIZIEUX CONTAY	26		Moved from VAUX-sur-SOMME 8.30 am. arriving at BAIZIEUX at 11.30 am. stood to till 5 pm. moved to CONTAY – arriving at 6.30 pm. Evacuated 14 sick animals to VII Corps V.E.S.	

D. D. & L., London, E.C. (A8001) Wt. W1771/M2031 750,000 5/17 Sch. 52 Forms/C2118/14

33rd Mobile Vet. Section

Army Form C. 2118.

WAR DIARY
or
~~INTELLIGENCE SUMMARY.~~
(Erase heading not required.)

Instructions regarding War Diaries and Intelligence Summaries are contained in F. S. Regs., Part II. and the Staff Manual respectively. Title pages will be prepared in manuscript.

March 1918

Place	Date	Hour	Summary of Events and Information	Remarks and references to Appendices
CONTAY	27		Paid men of section. Evacuated 6 sick animals to V.E.S.	
BAVELINCOURT	28		Left CONTAY 2.30 p.m. arrived at BAVELINCOURT 4 p.m. under shell fire. Evacuated 10 sick animals to VII Corps V.E.S.	
" "	29		Evacuated 21 sick animals to V.E.S. Pte WILKINS did not report back after acting as one of conducting party with this convoy. Section shelled with H.E. time bursts in morning & evening.	
" "	30		Evacuated 7 sick animals to V.E.S.	
CARDONNETTE	31		Left BAVELINCOURT at 6 a.m. reported to D.A.D.V.S. 21 Div at ALLONVILLE and went to CARDONNETTE at 9 a.m.	
			Date of Mobilization of 33rd M.V.S. April 1st 1915.	
			Proceeded overseas from U.K. Sept. 11th 1915.	
			[signature] Capt AVC. O.C. 33rd Mob. Vet. Sect.	

D. D. & L., London, E.C. (A8001) Wt. W1771/M2031 750,000 5/17 Sch. 52 Forms/C2118/14

33rd Mobile Vet. Section

Instructions regarding War Diaries and Intelligence Summaries are contained in F. S. Regs., Part II. and the Staff Manual respectively. Title pages will be prepared in manuscript.

WAR DIARY
or
~~INTELLIGENCE SUMMARY.~~
(Erase heading not required.)

Army Form C. 2118.

21

Vol 31

April 1918

Place	Date	Hour	Summary of Events and Information	Remarks and references to Appendices
CARDONNETTE	1st		Left CARDONNETTE 8 am. arrived at HANGEST at 3 P.M. & entrained at 9 P.M. from	
HANGEST			HANGEST Station.	
PESELHOEK	2nd		Arrived at PESELHOEK 1:30 pm. & detrained. Marched to LOCRE & formed	
LOCRE			billets in the Horse clipping camp at 5 pm.	
"	3rd		Nothing to report.	
"	4th		Left LOCRE 3 P.M. arrived at DRANOUTRE at 4 P.M.	
DRANOUTRE			PESELHOEK proceeded to V.E.S. 7th Corps.	
"	5th		Nothing to Report.	
"	6th		14 sick animals evacuated to V.E.S. 22nd Corps.	
"	7th		Nothing to report	
"	8th		do. do.	
"	9th		do. do.	
"	10th		Evacuated two sick animals (foot cases) to V.E.S. 22nd Corps. Destroyed one horse.	
			Paid men of section.	
	11th		Evacuated 10 sick animals to V.E.S. 22nd Corps.	
HERSKEN			Left DRANOUTRE & arrived HERSKEN near WESTOUTRE 11:15 am.	
"	12th		Nothing to report.	
"	13th		do. do.	
"	14th		do. do.	
"	15th		do. do.	

D. D. & L., London, E.C. (A8001) Wt. W1771/M2031 750,000 5/17 Sch. 52 Forms/C2118/14

33rd Mobile Vet Section

WAR DIARY
or
~~INTELLIGENCE SUMMARY.~~

(Erase heading not required.)

April 1918.

Instructions regarding War Diaries and Intelligence Summaries are contained in F. S. Regs., Part II. and the Staff Manual respectively. Title pages will be prepared in manuscript.

Army Form C. 2118.

Place	Date	Hour	Summary of Events and Information	Remarks and references to Appendices
HERSKEN	16th		Evacuated 45 sick animals to V.E.S. 22nd Corps. Left HERSKEN at	
WIPPENHOEK			7.50am. arrived WIPPENHOEK at 11 am	
"	17th		Pte Dunn reported back for duty from V.E.S. 7th Corps.	
"	18th		Nothing to report.	
"	19th		Evacuated 12 sick animals to 22nd Corps V.E.S.	
"	20th		Pte Keas reported back for duty from V.E.S. 7th Corps. Pte [illegible], Pte Bevan	
			+ Pte Usher reported for duty from No 15 [illegible]	
"	21st		Nothing to report.	
"	22nd		do. do	
"	23rd		Pte Long + Pte Morris reported for duty from [illegible]	
"	24th		Paid men of section	
"	25th		Evacuated 35 sick animals to V.E.S. 22nd Corps	
"	26th		Evacuated 22 sick animals to V.E.S. 22nd Corps	
			Pte Harris + Pte Pritchard proceeded to No 2 Vet Hospital [illegible]	
			A.V.C. [illegible]	
"	27th		Evacuated 5 sick animals to V.E.S. 9th Corps.	
"	28th		Nothing to report.	
"	29th		Evacuated 37 sick animals to V.E.S. 22nd Corps including [illegible] animals	
"	30th		Left WIPPENHOEK at 10 am. arrived in new camp at L 7 d 6 2 (sheet 27) south	
St JAN-TER-BIEZEN			west of St JAN-TER BIEZEN. at 11 am.	
			H. T. Sparrow Capt AVC	

D. D. & L., London, E.C. (A8004) Wt. W1771/M2031 750,000 5/17 Sch. 52 Forms/C2118/14

6

33rd Mobile Vet. Section
21st Divn
May 1917.

Instructions regarding War Diaries and Intelligence Summaries are contained in F. S. Regs., Part II. and the Staff Manual respectively. Title pages will be prepared in manuscript.

WAR DIARY
or
~~INTELLIGENCE SUMMARY.~~
(Erase heading not required.)

Army Form C. 2118.

Vol 30

Place	Date	Hour	Summary of Events and Information	Remarks and references to Appendices
near St Jan-ter-Biezen	1st		Evacuated 6 sick animals including 1 French horse to No. 2. V.E.S.	
LEDERZEELE	2nd		Left St Jan-ter-Biezen at 9 am. arrived LEDERZEELE at 5 p.m.	
	3rd		Nothing to report Evacuated 17 sick animals to 23rd Veterinary Hospital.	
ARQUES	4th		Left LEDERZEELE at 11 p.m. Arrived at ARQUES and entrained 3.30 a.m.	
	5th		Train left ARQUES station four hours later.	
In train. FERME de St ANTOINE near LAGERY	6th		Arrived at BOULEUSE at 4 p.m. After watering horses left for LAGERY and found good billets for men and horses at 6 p.m. at FERME de St ANTOINE	
	7th		Nothing to report.	
	8th		"	
	9th		"	
	10th			
	11th		Half of men of section were tested with tear gas and defective respirators changed. Paid men of section.	
	12th		Other half of men tested with tear gas.	
	13th		Nothing to report.	
VADIVILLE FARM near VAUX VARENNES	14th		Left LAGERY at 7 am. & arrived VADIVILLE Farm 1 Kilo S. of VAUX VARENNES at 4.30 p.m. Good billets and Veterinary Infirmary taken over from French	
	15th		Nothing to report.	
	16th		"	
	17th		"	

D. D. & L., London, E.C.
(A8001) Wt. W1771/M2031 750,000 5/17 Sch. 52 Forms/C2118/14

33rd Mobile Vet. Section
21st Division
May 1918.

Army Form C. 2118.

WAR DIARY
or
INTELLIGENCE SUMMARY.
(Erase heading not required.)

Instructions regarding War Diaries and Intelligence Summaries are contained in F. S. Regs., Part II. and the Staff Manual respectively. Title pages will be prepared in manuscript.

Place	Date	Hour	Summary of Events and Information	Remarks and references to Appendices
VADIVILLE FARM.	18th		Nothing to report.	
	19th		Evacuated 36 sick animals to 9th V.E.S.	
	20th		Nothing to report	
	21st		"	
	22nd		"	
	23rd		"	
	24th		Evacuated 11 Sick Animals and sent 2 hides to 9th V.E.S.	
			Sent advance party to new camp at BOIS de CUISSAT to take over from French and clean and disinfect place, which was used as a Veterinary Infirmary.	
	25th		Sent more men to help clean camp.	
Bois de CUISSAT.	26th		Section moved at 10 am. to new camp at Bois de CUISSAT arrived at 11:30 am.	
	27th		Gas and shell bombardment from 2 am. till 5 pm. from Germans. No casualties	
			Paid men of Section.	
ROSNAY	28th		Left CUISSAT CAMP 5 am. arriving at ROSNAY 9:30 am. Left 12 noon and arrived in VILLE en TARDENOIS at 2:30 pm.	
VILLE en TARDENOIS	29th		Left VILLE en TARDENOIS at 9.0 am. arrived La NEUVILLE 2 pm.	
LA NEUVILLE	30th		Left LA NEUVILLE 3 am. arrived FORET d'EPERNAY 3:30 pm.	
	31st		Left FORET d'EPERNAY 11 am. arriving at SOULIÈRES at 5:30 pm.	

[signature]
Capt. A.V.C.

D. D. & L., London, E.C.
(A8001) Wt. W1771/M2031 750,000 3/17 Sch. 52 Forms/C2118/14

1 33rd Mobile Vet. Section **WAR DIARY** ~~or~~ Army Form C. 2118.

~~**INTELLIGENCE SUMMARY.**~~

(Erase heading not required.)

Instructions regarding War Diaries and Intelligence Summaries are contained in F. S. Regs., Part II. and the Staff Manual respectively. Title pages will be prepared in manuscript.

June 1918

Vol 34

Place	Date	Hour	Summary of Events and Information	Remarks and references to Appendices
SOULIÈRES	June 1st	—	Nothing to Report	
"	2nd	—	" " "	
	3rd	—	Left SOULIÈRES at 10 am. arrived at COURJEONNET at 4·30 P.M.	
COURJEONNET	4th	—	Nothing to report.	
—	5th	—	" " "	
—	6th	—	" " "	
—	7th	—	" " "	
—	8th	—	" " "	
—	9th	—	Evacuated 4 sick animals sent 1 hide to 9 V.E.S. Left COURJEONNET 11 am. arrived at VERDEY 4·30 P.M	
VERDEY MOEURS	10th		Left VERDEY at 10 am. arriving at MOEURS at 11 am.	
	11th		Paid men of Section.	
	12th		Nothing to Report.	
FERE-CHAMPENOISE	13th		Left MOEURS 2·30 p.m. arrived 4 Kilos S. of FÈRE-CHAMPENOISE at 9·45 p.m. via CORROY.	
	14th		Left this camp at 11 am. arrived at Station of FERE-CHAMPENOISE ~~at 1 am.~~ Section entrained 2 pm. and train left at 5·15 pm	
PONT de REMY	15th		Detrained at PONT de REMY near ABBEVILLE at 3 p.m. and marched to CERISY-BULEUX arriving at 8 P.M.	
CERISY-BULEUX.	16th		Nothing to Report.	
—	17th		" " "	
—	18th		" " "	

D. D. & L., London, E.C.
(A8001) Wt. W1771/M2031 750,000 5/17 Sch. 52 Forms/C2118/14

33rd Mobile Vet. Section

Instructions regarding War Diaries and Intelligence Summaries are contained in F. S. Regs., Part II. and the Staff Manual respectively. Title pages will be prepared in manuscript.

WAR DIARY

~~or~~

~~INTELLIGENCE SUMMARY.~~

(*Erase heading not required.*)

Army Form C. 2118.

June 1918.

Place	Date	Hour	Summary of Events and Information	Remarks and references to Appendices
CERISY-BULEUX.	June 19th	—	Evacuated sick horses to No 14 Vet. Hosp.	
—	20th		Routine duties	
—	21st			
BAROMESNIL	22nd		Left CERISY-BULEUX at 8 am. arrived at BAROMESNIL at 5.30 P.M.	
—	23rd		Nothing to Report.	
—	24th		— — —	
—	25th		— — —	
—	26th		Evacuated sick horses to No. 14. Vet. Hosp.	
—	27th		Paid men of Section.	
—	28th		Evacuated 44 sick animals to No 14 Vet. Hosp.	
—	29th		Routine duties.	
OISEMONT.	30th		Left BAROMESNIL 2 P.M. arrived at OISEMONT 9 P.M.	

[illegible] Capt. A.V.C.

D. D. & L., London, E.C.
(A8001) Wt. W1771/M2031 750,000 5/17 Sch. 52 Forms/C2118/14

19 21

Army Form C. 2118.

33rd Mobile Vet Section **WAR DIARY** or ~~INTELLIGENCE SUMMARY~~.

(Erase heading not required.)

Instructions regarding War Diaries and Intelligence Summaries are contained in F. S. Regs., Part II. and the Staff Manual respectively. Title pages will be prepared in manuscript.

July 1918.

V.A. 35

Place	Date	Hour	Summary of Events and Information	Remarks and references to Appendices
OISEMONT	July 1st		Left OISEMONT at 8 am. arrived at BOURDON at 3·30 P.M.	
BOURDON	2nd		Left BOURDON at 9 am. arrived at CANAPLES at 1 30 pm.	
CANAPLES	3rd		Left CANAPLES at 3·30 am. arrived at RAINCHEVAL at 9 am.	
RAINCHEVAL	4th		Routine duties.	
"	5th		Evacuated 24 sick animals to No. 5. V.E.S. & 2 hides.	
"	6th		Nothing to report.	
"	7th		" " "	
"	8th		Evacuated 15 sick animals to No. 5 V.E.S.	
"	9th		Paid men of Section.	
"	10th		All section had their box respirators tested in a gas chamber. Box respirators worn for one hour on normal work ~~as a~~ for instruction & experience	
"	11th		" " " " " " " " " " " " "	
"	12th		" " " " " " " " " " " " "	
"	13th		" " " " " " " " " "	
			Evacuated 33 sick animals to No. 5 V.E.S. & 1 hide.	
"	14.		N.T.R.	
"	15.		N.T.R	
"	16		Evacuated 2 sick animals & sent 2 hides to No 5. V.E.S.	
"	17		Routine duties.	
"	18		Evacuated 16 sick animals.	
"	19		Routine duties.	

D. D. & L., London, E.C.
(A8001) Wt. W1771/M2031 750,000 5/17 Sch. 52 Forms/C2118/14

33rd Mobile Vet. Sect.

Instructions regarding War Diaries and Intelligence Summaries are contained in F. S. Regs., Part II. and the Staff Manual respectively. Title pages will be prepared in manuscript.

WAR DIARY

~~or~~

~~INTELLIGENCE SUMMARY.~~

(Erase heading not required.)

July, 1918

Army Form C. 2118.

Place	Date	Hour	Summary of Events and Information	Remarks and references to Appendices
Raincheval	July 20		Corpl. Levie proceeded on leave to Paris	
"	21		Evacuated 11 sick animals to No 5 V.E.S.	
"	22		Routine duties.	
"	23		Evacuated 21 sick animals [illegible] No 5 V.E.S.	
"	24		Nothing to report.	
"	25		Evacuated sick animals to No. 5 V.E.S.	
"	26		Nothing to report.	
"	27		Paid men of Section	
"	28		Routine duties.	
"	29		"	
"	30		Evacuated 9 animals to No 5 V.E.S. Pte Bevan proceeded on leave to U.K.	
	31		Nothing to report.	

H. D. [illegible]
Capt.

D. D. & L., London, E.C.
(A8001) Wt. W1771/M2031 750,000 5/17 Sch. 52 Forms/C2118/14

33rd Mobile Veterinary Section

WAR DIARY
or
INTELLIGENCE SUMMARY.
(Erase heading not required.)

33rd Mob Vet Sec.

Army Form C. 2118.

Instructions regarding War Diaries and Intelligence Summaries are contained in F. S. Regs., Part II. and the Staff Manual respectively. Title pages will be prepared in manuscript.

May 1917.

Vol 21

Place	Date	Hour	Summary of Events and Information	Remarks and references to Appendices
BOISLEUX au MONT	1st		Evacuated to Base Hospital from Supply railhead Sixty two Sick Animals. Also seven hides	
"	2nd		nothing to report	
"	3rd		"	
"	4th		Evacuated Seventeen sick animals to base and four hides	
"	5th		nothing to report	
"	6th		Received a new horse float.	
"	7th		nothing to report	
"	8th		Evacuated twenty four sick animals to base also eight hides	
"	9th		nothing to report	
"	10th		"	
"	11th		Evacuated twenty five Sick Animals to base also three hides	
"	12th		Left BOISLEUX au MONT 10 am arrived ADINFER 11.30 am	
ADINFER	13th		nothing to report	
	14th		nothing to report	
	15		nothing to report	
	16th		nothing to report	

T2134. Wt. W708—776. 500000. 4/15. Sir J. C. & S.

7

33 Mobile Veterinary Section 21

Army Form C. 2118.

WAR DIARY
or
INTELLIGENCE SUMMARY.

(Erase heading not required.)

Instructions regarding War Diaries and Intelligence Summaries are contained in F. S. Regs., Part II. and the Staff Manual respectively. Title pages will be prepared in manuscript.

Vol 36

Place	Date	Hour	Summary of Events and Information	Remarks and references to Appendices
RAINCHEVAL.	August	1st	27 Animals evacuated to No V.E.S.	
" "	"	2nd	Nothing to report.	
" "	"	3rd	Corporal Levie. C.W. returned from Paris leave.	
" "	"	4th	Evacuated 32 Sick animals to No 5 V.E.S.	
" "	"	5th	Nothing to report.	
" "	"	6th	Evacuated 27 sick animals to No 5 V.E.S.	
" "	"	7th	Nothing to report.	
" "	"	8th	Evacuated 7 sick animals and 3 Hides to No 5 V.E.S.	
" "	"	9th	Nothing to report.	
" "	"	10th	Nothing to report.	
" "	"	11th	Evacuated 21 sick animals to No 5 V.E.S.	
" "	"	12th	Pte Ainsworth proceed on leave. to U.K.	
" "	"	13th	Evacuated 23 sick animals to No 5 V.E.S.	
" "	"	14th	Nothing to report.	
" "	"	15th	Evacuated 15 Sick animals to No 5 V.E.S.	
" "	"	16th	Nothing to report.	
" "	"	17th	Driver Holliday admitted to Hospital.	
" "	"	18th	Evacuated 25 sick animals to No 5 V. E. S.	
" "	"	19th	Evacuated 1 sick animal to No 5 V.E.S.	
" "	"	20th	Evacuated 29 sick animals to No 5 V.E.S.	
" "	"	21st	Pte Morville J.B. wounded by bomb, also 2 horses of section.	
" "	"	22nd	Evacuated 14 sick animals and 2 hides to No 5 V.E.S.	
" "	"	23rd	Nothing to report.	
" "	"	24th	Nothing to report.	
MAILLY MAILLET	"	25th	Arrived here. Two men arrived from base. → Evacuated 12 sick animals to No 5 V.E.S.	
" "	"	30th	Captain Sparrow, A.V.C. O.C. M.V.S. proceeded on leave. Captain Hadfield A.V.C. took over Section.	
GRANDCOURT	"	31st	Arrived here.. Corporal Levie left for No 2 Veterinary Hospital HAVRE.	

R W Hadfield
Captain, A.V.C.
for O.C. 33rd Mobile Veterinary Section.

D. D. & L., London, E.C.
(A8004) Wt. W1771/M1-31 750,000 5/17 Sch. 52 Forms/C2118/14

29 21

Instructions regarding War Diaries and Intelligence Summaries are contained in F. S. Regs., Part II, and the Staff Manual respectively. Title pages will be prepared in manuscript.

WAR DIARY
or
~~INTELLIGENCE SUMMARY.~~
(Erase heading not required.)

Army Form C. 2118.

33rd Mob Vet Sec
Sept 1918
VS 37

Place	Date	Hour	Summary of Events and Information	Remarks and references to Appendices
Grandcourt	Sept 1		Pte Ginham proceeded on leave. Evacuated 15 Sick Animals & 1 Hide to 5th Corps V E S	
"	" 2		N.T.R.	
"	" 3		Evacuated 12 Animals & 3 Hides to 5 Corps V E S	
"	" 4		Pte Keighley returned from leave.	
"	" 5		Evacuated 3 Horses to 5 Corps V E S one horse Destroyed. Sgt James proceeded on leave. Left Grandcourt 11 AM arrived Le Sars 1 PM	
Le Sars	" 6		Left Le Sars at 3 30 PM arrived at Beaulencourt 5 30 PM	
Beaulencourt	" 7		Paid men of Section.	
"	" 8		Evacuated 8 Sick Horses to 4th Corps V E S & 1 Hide. Pte Hellens proceeded on leave.	
"	" 9		N.T.R.	
"	" 10		Evacuated 11 sick Animals to No 5 V E S	
"	" 11		N.T.R.	
"	" 12		Evacuated 3 Horses & 6 Mules to No 5 Corps V E S. Pte Usher returned from leave.	
"	" 13		1 Horse Destroyed. ~~Pte Fletcher returned from leave~~	
"	" 14		1 Hide received	
"	" 15		Evacuated 12 Sick Horses to 5 V E S Left Beaulencourt at 10 AM, arriving at Le Mesnil 11 30 AM.	
Le Mesnil	" 16		Capt Sparrow returned from leave.	
"	" 17		Evacuated 11 Horses & 7 Mules also 1 Hide to 5 Corps V E S	
"	" 18		Private Ginham returned from leave. Pte Collins returned to duty with Section	
"	" 19		Evacuated 11 Horses & 5 Mules to 5th Corps V E S also 2 Hides	
"	" 20		Evacuated 1 Float Case to 5th Corps V E S in morning & 16 Captured German Horses in afternoon	
"	" 21		Evacuated 1 Horse (Float Case) also 10 Horses & 5 Mules to 5th Corps V E S 5 Hides to 5 V E S Pte Saul proceeded on leave	
"	" 22		Evacuated 1 Horse (Float Case) to 5 V E S	
"	" 23		Evacuated 1 Float Case to 5 V E S Paid men of Section	
"	" 24		Evacuated 1 Float Case also 13 Horses & 2 Mules to No 5 V E S	
"	" 25		N.T.R.	
"	" 26		Evacuated 1 Horse (Float Case) to 5 Corps V E S. Pte Hellens returned from leave. Pte Jacques returned to unit	
"	" 27		N.T.R.	
"	" 28		Evacuated 15 Horses 1 Mule & 3 Hides to 5 V E S	
"	" 29		Left Le Mesnil at 1 PM arriving at Equancourt at 2 30 PM Evacuated 7 Horses to 5 V E S also 3 Hides	
Equancourt	" 30		N.T.R.	

[signature] Captain
O.C. 33rd Mobile Vety Section

31

No 39

1

C O N F I D E N T I A L.

WAR DIARY

33rd Mobile Veterinary Section.

October 1st - 31st 1918.

33rd Mobile Vet. Section

Sheet I

Army Form C. 2118.

WAR DIARY
~~or~~
~~INTELLIGENCE SUMMARY.~~
(Erase heading not required.)

Instructions regarding War Diaries and Intelligence Summaries are contained in F. S. Regs., Part II. and the Staff Manual respectively. Title pages will be prepared in manuscript.

October 1918.

Place	Date	Hour	Summary of Events and Information	Remarks and references to Appendices
EQUANCOURT	1st		Routine duties	
"	2nd		" "	
"	3rd		Evacuated 7 horses & 3 mules to No.5 V.E.S.	
"	4th		Evacuated 22 horses & 2 mules to No 5 V.E.S.	
"	5th		Pte P. Long proceeded on leave to U.K. from 7th to 21st inst	
			Evacuated 7 horses to No 5. V.E.S. Pte Crampton & Pte Welch returned to No. 2 Coy. Train	
"	6th		Nothing to report.	
GOUZEAUCOURT	7th		Left EQUANCOURT at 9.30 am. arriving at ~~ABBU~~ GOUZEAUCOURT at 11 am.	
			Pte Collings left for leave in France from 8–17th Evacuated animals to No 5 V.E.S.	
"	8th		Sgt. James returned from leave	
"	9th		Evacuated 22 horses & 11 mules to No 5 V.E.S.	
"	10th		Evacuated 10 horses & 4 mules to No 5 V.E.S. Pte Saul returned from leave.	
BANTOUZELLE			Left GOUZEAUCOURT at 9.30 am, arriving at BANTOUZELLE at 12 pm.	
WALINCOURT	11th		Left ~~WALINCOURT~~ BANTOUZELLE at 10 am. arriving at WALINCOURT at 2 pm.	
"			Evacuated 7 horses (HD) & 1 mule to No. 5 V.E.S.	
"	12th		Nothing to Report	
	13th		" "	
"	14th		Evacuated 11 horses & 2 mules to No. 5 V.E.S.	
"	15th		Nothing to Report	
"	16th		Pte Aisthorpe returned to unit.	

D. D. & L., London, E.C.
(A8004) Wt. W1771/M2731 750,000 5/17 Sch. 52 Forms/C2118/14

33rd Mobile Vet. Section

Sheet II

Army Form C. 2118.

Instructions regarding War Diaries and Intelligence Summaries are contained in F. S. Regs., Part II. and the Staff Manual respectively. Title pages will be prepared in manuscript.

WAR DIARY
or
INTELLIGENCE SUMMARY.
(Erase heading not required.)

October 1918

Place	Date	Hour	Summary of Events and Information	Remarks and references to Appendices
WALINCOURT	17th		Evacuated 14 horses & 3 mules to No. 5 V.E.S.	
"	18th		L/Cpl. Fazgett proceeds on leave to U.K. from 21st Oct. to 4th Nov. Evacuated 1 float case	
"	19th		Nothing to report.	
"	20th		Pte Collings returned from leave.	
"	21st		Evacuated 18 horses & 1 mule to No. 5 V.E.S.	
MONTIGNY	22nd		Left WALINCOURT at 9.30 am arriving at MONTIGNY at 12.30 pm.	
"	23rd		Evacuated sick horses to No. 5 V.E.S.	
INCHY	24th		Left MONTIGNY at 7.45 am. arriving at INCHY at 10 am.	
"			Evacuated 10 sick horses & 5 mules to No. 5 V.E.S.	
	25th		Pte Debenham proceeded on leave to U.K. Oct. 28th to Nov. 11th	
			Pte Alvey 1st Lincolns attached temporarily to section.	
			Evacuated 4 sick animals to No. 5 V.E.S.	
"	26th		Evacuated 1 float case, also 5 horses & 4 mules to No. 5 V.E.S.	
"	27th		Despatched 1 float case to No. 5 V.E.S. Pte Dickson returned to No. 4 Coy 21st Divl Train	
"	28th		Evacuated 9 horses & 1 mule to No. 5 V.E.S.	
"	29th		1 wounded mule destroyed & distributed for use of civilians of INCHY.	
NEUVILLY			Left Inchy at 9.15 am arriving at NEUVILLY at 11 am.	
"	30th		Pte Fulker A.S.C. proceeded on special leave to U.K. from November 2nd to 16th inst.	
			Pte P. Long not yet returned from leave, & report of absence sent to D.A.D.V.S. 21st Divn.	

D. D. & L., London, E.C. (A8004) Wt. W1771/M2-31 750,000 5/17 Sch. 52 Forms/C2118/14

33rd Mobile Vet Section **WAR DIARY** *or* **INTELLIGENCE SUMMARY.** Sheet VII

Army Form C. 2118.

Instructions regarding War Diaries and Intelligence Summaries are contained in F. S. Regs., Part II. and the Staff Manual respectively. Title pages will be prepared in manuscript.

October 1918. (*Erase heading not required.*)

Place	Date	Hour	Summary of Events and Information	Remarks and references to Appendices
NEUVILLY	31st		Evacuated 7 horses & 3 mules to No. 5 V.E.S. Destroyed 1 wounded mule for civilians of Neuvilly. Pte R Race No. 5777 14th N.F.(P) temporarily attached to M.V.S.	

H. D. Sparrow Capt. A.V.C.

D. D. & L., London, E.C. (A6004) Wt. W1771/M2-31 750,000 5/17 Sch. 52 Forms/C2118/14

17 21

9/8 40

C O N F I D E N T I A L.

WAR DIARY

OF

33rd Mobile Veterinary Section.

FROM:- 1st November 1918. TO:- 30th November 1918.

33rd Mobile Vet Section

Sheet I

WAR DIARY

or

~~INTELLIGENCE SUMMARY.~~

(Erase heading not required.)

Army Form C. 2118.

Instructions regarding War Diaries and Intelligence Summaries are contained in F. S. Regs., Part II. and the Staff Manual respectively. Title pages will be prepared in manuscript.

Nov. 1918.

No. 33 MOBILE VETERINARY SECTION No. .... Date ....

Place	Date	Hour	Summary of Events and Information	Remarks and references to Appendices
NEUVILLY	1st		Routine duties.	
"	2nd		Evacuated four horses & destroyed one which was distributed amongst the civilians. Pte R. Ruce 14th N.F.s returned to unit	
"	3rd		Evacuated 28 animals to no 5 V.E.S. Destroyed two horses. Evacuated 1 mule (afloat case) and two hides to no. 29 M.V.S.	
"	4th		Evacuated 14 horses & 1 mule to no. 5 V.E.S. and 1 horse afloat case & 2 hides to no. 29 M.V.S	
"	5th		Evacuated 7 horses & 1 mule to no 5 V.E.S.	
POIX du NORD			Left NEUVILLY at 9.15 am arriving at POIX du NORD at 1-15pm	
" LOCQUIGNOL	6th		Left POIX du NORD at 2 pm arriving at LOCQUIGNOL at 5 PM. Major Macdonald & Pte Lambert ASC. & Pte Tracey X Hussars & Pte Oldfield 1st Lincolns attached to M.V.S.	
"	7th		Routine duties.	
"	8th		" "	
"	9th		Pte W. Fletcher AVC. proceeded to no. 2 Vet Hosp. for transfer to Home Establishment on account of age. Pte H.B. Paramore proceeded on leave to U.K from 11th-25th Nov.	
LA GRANDE CARRIÈRE			Left LOCQUIGNOL at 9.30 am, arrived at LE GRAND CARRIÈRE at 12 am. Evacuated 13 animals to no 5 V.E.S.	

D. D. & L., London, E.C. (A8004) Wt. W1771/M2-31 750,000 5/17 Sch. 52 Forms/C2118/14

33rd Mobile Vet. Section **WAR DIARY** ~~or~~ ~~INTELLIGENCE SUMMARY.~~ Sheet II

Army Form C. 2118.

Instructions regarding War Diaries and Intelligence Summaries are contained in F. S. Regs., Part II. and the Staff Manual respectively. Title pages will be prepared in manuscript.

(Erase heading not required.)

Nov 1918

Place	Date	Hour	Summary of Events and Information	Remarks and references to Appendices
LEGRAND CARRIÈRE	Nov. 10th		L/Cpl Targett + Pte P. Long returned from leave. Paid men of section	
"	11th		Pte Alvey returned to 1st Lincs. 1 mule destroyed & distributed to civilians. L/Cpl Targett promoted to A/Acting Cpl from Aug 31st to replace P/Cpl Levie transferred to base for infantry. Order received that hostility cease at 11 am.	
"	12th		Routine duties.	
"	13th		Evacuated 31 animals to 5th Corps V.E.S.	
	14th		Pte Debenham returned from leave. Evac 7 animals to 5th Corps V.E.S.	
	15th		Capt Sparrow left for special to U.K. from 20-11-18 to 4-12-18. Capt Pindar took command of section.	
	16th		Evacuated 8 animals to No 4 V.E.S. Major Macdonald. Pte Oldfield & Tracey rejoined 21st Div Hd Qrs.	
	17th		Pte Lambert returned to Hd Qrs 21st Div. Pte Saul admitted to 64th Fld Amb	
	18th		Four Stray animals issued to 1st East Yorks.	
	19th		Routine duties	
	20th		Evacuated 9 animals to 4th Corps V.E.S.	
	21st		Evacuated Charger belonging to Major Hopkins to 5th Corps V.E.S. by Motor Float	
	22nd		Evac 5 animals to 4th Corps V.E.S. also 5 Hides	
	23rd		Two Stray mules issued to 9th K.O.Y.L.I. also 2 L.D. issued to 1st East Yorks.	

D. D. & L., London, E.C. (A8001) Wt. W1771/M2031 750,000 5/17 Sch. 52 Forms/C2118/14

Instructions regarding War Diaries and Intelligence Summaries are contained in F. S. Regs., Part II. and the Staff Manual respectively. Title pages will be prepared in manuscript.

33rd Mobile Vety Section

Nov 1918.

WAR DIARY
~~or~~
~~INTELLIGENCE SUMMARY.~~
(Erase heading not required.)

Army Form C. 2118.

Sheet III

Place	Date Novr	Hour	Summary of Events and Information	Remarks and references to Appendices
LE-GRAND CARRIERE	24th		Routine duties	
" "	25th		Evacuated 8 animals to 4th Corps V.E.S.	
" "	26th		Dr Fulker reported back from leave.	
" "	27th		Cpl Targett proceeded to AILLY-SUR-SOMME to make arrangements for billets for Section. Cpl Craig proceeded on leave to U.K. from 30.11.18 to 14.12.18.	
" "			Paid men of Section	
" "	28th		Routine duties	
" "	29th		Pte Paramore returned from leave. Capt. Rindar A.V.C. Ptes. Welch and Crampton 1st Lincolns attached to Section temporarily.	
" "	30th		Routine duties.	

No. 33 MOBILE VETERINARY SECTION
No.
Date

E. J. [illegible] Capt. A.V.C.
for O.C. 33rd M.V.S.

D. D. & L., London, E.C. (A8001) Wt. W1771/M2031 750,000 5/17 Sch. 52 Forms/C2118/14

19

21

C O N F I D E N T I A L.

WAR DIARY

OF

33rd Mobile Veterinary Section R.A.V.C.

FROM:- December 1st. TO:- December 31st 1918.

Instructions regarding War Diaries and Intelligence Summaries are contained in F. S. Regs., Part II. and the Staff Manual respectively. Title pages will be prepared in manuscript.

Sheet 1.

WAR DIARY
or
INTELLIGENCE SUMMARY.

December 1918. *(Erase heading not required.)*

33rd Mobile Vety Section

Army Form C. 2118.

Place	Date	Hour	Summary of Events and Information	Remarks and references to Appendices
LA GRANDE CARRIERE	1st		Routine Duties	
"	2nd		Evacuated 3 Horses & 3 Mules to No 4 V.E.S. Pte J Rees proceeded on leave	
"	3rd		N.T.R	
"	4th		N.T.R	
"	5th		N.T.R	
"	6th		Evacuated 3 Horses & 2 Mules to No 4 V.E.S	
"	7th		Capt. Sparrow returned from leave	
"	8th		Pte Sales 201276. 1 Lincs attached temporarily	
"	9th		N.T.R	
"	10th		Capt. Sparrow left the section, transferred to No 5 V.E.S	
"	11th		N.T.R	
"	12th		Lieut. Ley R.A.V.C. and Pte Gillick T. 30412 R.A.V.C attached temporarily Pte J. T. Jackson 12013 1 Lincoln attached temporarily	
"	13th		N.T.R	
"	14th		Evacuated 1 Horse & 1 Mule to 49th M.V.S. 32nd Div	
"	15th		N.T.R	
"	16th		Despatched 1 Horse & 3 Mules to 49th M.V.S. Pte Sales 1 Lincs returned to unit.	
"	17th		Left LA GRANDE CARRIERE at 7.30 AM arriving at OVILLIERS at 1. P.M	
OVILLIERS	18th		Left OVILLIERS at 7.30 AM arriving at INCHY BEAUMOND at 11 AM Corpl Craig arrived from leave at AILLY-sur-Somme.	
INCHY BEAUMONT	19th		Left INCHY BEAUMONT at 8 AM arriving at AUBENCHEUL at 1 PM	
AUBENCHEUL	20th		Left AUBENCHEUL at 8.10 AM arriving at BUIRE at 1. P.M	
BUIRE	21st		Left BUIRE at 7.40 AM arriving at PROYART at 2.15 P.M	
PROYART	22nd		Left PROYART at 7.20 AM arriving at GLISY at 1.15 P.M	
GLISY	23		Left GLISY at 7.15 AM arriving at AILLY-SUR-SOMME at 11 A.M.	

No. 33 MOBILE VETERINARY SECTION No. ...... Date ......

D. D. & L., London, E.C. (A8001) Wt. W1771/M2031 750,000 5/17 Sch. 52 Forms/C2118/14

Army Form C. 2118.

WAR DIARY
or
INTELLIGENCE SUMMARY.
(Erase heading not required.)

Instructions regarding War Diaries and Intelligence Summaries are contained in F. S. Regs., Part II. and the Staff Manual respectively. Title pages will be prepared in manuscript.

Sheet 2.

December 1918

33rd Mobile Vety Section

Place	Date	Hour	Summary of Events and Information	Remarks and references to Appendices
AILLY-SUR-SOMME	24th		Pte Rice E.B. No 214 RAVC arrived from LE HAVRE to be attached to Section. Evacuated 17 Horses to No 5 V.E.S.	
"	25th		Paid Men of Section.	
"	26th		Pte J Brooks 14 N.F. (Pioneers) proceeded on leave.	
"	27th		Evacuated 5 Horses & 3 Mules to No 5 V.E.S. Pte J Rees 8552 R.A.V.C returned from leave.	
"	28th		N.T.R	
"	29th		Pte H LONG to Hospital. Pte G Mack J. 30412 R.A.V.C. proceeded to No 13 Vety Hosp. Left AILLY-sur-SOMME at 11 AM arriving at DREUIL at 11.30 AM.	
DREUIL	30th		N.T.R	
"	31st		Lieut Gay and Pte Welch 1st Lincs to be attached to No 2 Coy. Div Train. Evacuated 16 Horses & 1 Mule to No 5 V.E.S.	

No. 33 MOBILE VETERINARY SECTION
No. ....
Date 1/1/19.

E S P[illegible]
Capt RAVC
O.C. 33 Mobile Vety Secn

Copy of letter from Major S.J.Chittenden.

to General Sir Hubert Gough.

238, Hornby Road.
Blackpool.
7th August 1931.

PRIVATE & CONFIDENTIAL.

TO: General Sir Hubert Gough GCMG.KCB.KCVO.

Dear Sir Hubert,

I trust that you will pardon the liberty I take in addressing you personally, the only justification I can offer is my keen desire to thank you with every sincerity for the extracts from your Memoirs now appearing in the "Daily Telegraph."

If, in the multitude of more important correspondence, you should find time to read the following, you will perhaps more readily understand how greatly I do appreciate the fact that daylight has at last been allowed to illuminate the somewhat tangled versions of what took place in March 1918.

My humble part in those momentous times was that of Company Commander to "D" Company, 21st M.G.Battn. or as were better known before the reorganisation, 237th M.G. which was the 21st Division Commander's M.G. reserve.

It is when I know what happened, on my little bit of front starting at Epehy, that I have for years hoped that you would feel constrained to vindicate those who fought with you against very heavy odds and to the limit of their ability, did their job.

My unit was taken out of the line on the 18th March and put into Divisional Reserve, and on the outbreak of the German barrage on that foggy morning of the 21st I was ordered to establish contact with the centre Brigade Commander just behind Epehy and strengthen the line where necessary. That Brigade was the 110th (Leicesters) under Lord Loch. As you have said we held on until the next day, when owing to the prior retirement of the 9th Division from Hendecort and the 16th from Ronssoy - Lempire, we were almost cut off and had to extricate ourselves in a carefully prepared movement.

Our casualties had been very severe; but we settled down as best we could with the only infantry we could find - namely oddments and a battalions of the 1/Herts, under a Colonel Phillips at the rear of Templeux le Foss on the night of the 22nd. During the night Colonel Settle (commanding 21st M.G,Battn.) came round and after inspecting our dispositions for General Campbell, made an appointment with me for 5 a.m. at Haut Allaine. Colonel Settle was not there for the appointment at 5 o'clock - which I kept after leaving things as organised as possible in the circumstances in the line which we had established, I found instead that, we were being outflanked from the direction of Peronne and so the artillery and all transport was hastening away at dawn both from Haut Allaines and Moislaines. I remember seeing the 39th M.G.Battn. or a part of it, and from Capt. Mowatt an old friend of mine, borrowing a horse, so that I could get ahead to find Colonel Seattle and re-establish contact and keep touch with what guns I had left.

I found the Colonel at Clery sur Somme having lunch with the Div.Commander - picnic fashion, and I believe I was able to tell them the chief points in the withdrawal which I could see had taken place since the fog had lifted.

My orders then were to proceed to Mariecourt and collect what guns, ammunition etc, I could find together with as many men as possible from the 21st Bn.stragglers and (acting as 2nd-in-command i/c Battn. Major Borthwick having been wounded and evacuated) return to Clery. I succeeded in finding some of the battalion transport together with stragglers, and by the old process of scrounging managed to get 4 guns in various states of repair and plenty of ammunition from a motor M.G. unit and returned to Clery. I had collected 47 N.C.O's and men and when I arrived at Clery the Colonel had a little garrison of 31 all ranks. We proceeded through the night to make a strong position which would guard a road, a valley and a bridge over the river (Somme). An infantry battalion joined us in the night but withdrew before dawn, and a Canadian motor M.G. unit came and looked at us and then went back and so we faced the morning 78 strong, plus Colonel Settle, Capt. Pope and the Adjutant and myself.

We had the most admirable shooting but after some hours of shelling the Germans worked behind us in two places and we were bombed by T.M.shells and M.G.fire from two rear positions and shelled from the ffont. The end was inevitable, one by one this garrison dwindled down - the Colonel was killed, the Adjutant was killed, and eventually I found myself alone all but for my runner - who went in one direction and I in another to see if we could find anyone left in our scattered little posts to get together. Whilst engaged in this I was blown off my feet by a T.M.shell and was next aware of the world when my runner tried to get me up and told me that the Germans had passed over us and were a good mile on. I just had time to destroy my remaining papers when a party of Germans came on us and we were just collected after resisting until nearly 4 p.m. (24th).

So far as I am aware, that runner and myself are the only two alive of that garrison with the exception of Capt. Enright, my second-in-command, who was fighting in the rear of us and who also eventually was captured.

My old company when withdrawn consisted of 1 officer and 14 other ranks - chiefly details, and nearly 75 per cent of the remainder were killed. It is when I think of these lads that I rejoice that the truth about the Fifth Army and what it accomplished against overwhelming odds, has at last been made public.

I have taken this liberty of troubling you with these

long-winded details for three reasons -

1. Because my four hectic days in touch with the Germans on that occasion give me at least the right to support you with gratitude in your account of what took place.

2. There is an outside chance that I may have mentioned something of interest in the movements of units at that time.

3. To be able to assert that given adequate support, the 9th and 16th Divisions could have held their line as the 21st did, and that sector held by the VII.Corps would have inflicted very serious casualties on the Germans with the loss of no ground of any importance, if you had been properly treated with sufficient reserves to have enabled you to undertake the stupendous task allotted to you. If you will forgive my presumption in saying so.

May I in conclusion ask whether, when your Memoirs are published, you will have the kindness to autograph any copies sent to you by any surviving members of the Fifth Army, as I know that, personally, I should be as very proud to possess that as I was to be allowed to hold my very humble post on that never-to-be-forgotten spring morning.

With renewed thanks, Sir, for your plain spoken articles.

I beg to remain,

Yours faithfully,

(sgd) S.J.Chittenden.
late Major. M.G.Corps.

19

21

VR 42

21 Div

C O N F I D E N T I A L.

W A R   D I A R Y.

OF

33rd Mobile Veterinary Section., R.A.V.C.

FROM;- 1st January 1919.   TO:- 31st January 1919.

Instructions regarding War Diaries and Intelligence Summaries are contained in F. S. Regs., Part II. and the Staff Manual respectively. Title pages will be prepared in manuscript.

Sheet 1.

WAR DIARY
or
INTELLIGENCE SUMMARY.
(Erase heading not required.)

33rd Mobile Vety Sec.

January 1919.

Army Form C. 2118.

Place	Date	Hour	Summary of Events and Information	Remarks and references to Appendices
DREUIL	1st		Routine Duties.	
"	2nd		Evacuated 12 Horses & 3 Mules to No 5 V. E. S.	
"	3rd		Routine Duties	
"	4th		Evacuated 12 Horses & 1 Mule to No 5 V. E. S.	
"	5		Routine Duties.	
"	6th		Evacuated 10 Horses & 1 Mule to No 5 V. E. S. S. Cte. [illegible] returned to Unit. Sergeants Townsend W. TT/01358 & Jackson H. L. TT/01071 arrived from No. 2 Vety Hospital.	
"	7th		Evacuated 11 Horses & 1 Mule to No 5 V. E. S.	
"	8th		Paid men of Section.	
"	9th		Routine Duties.	
"	10th		Do Do	
"	11th		Sgts James & Butcher left the Section for No 2 Vety Hospital. Have	
"			Evacuated 9 Horses & 3 Mules to No 5 V. E. S.	
"	12th		N.T.R.	
"	13th		Routine Duties	
"	14th		Do Do	
"	15th		Evacuated Eight horses & 1 Mule to No 5 V. E. S.	
"	16th		Routine Duties.	
"	17th		Evacuated 1 Float Case to No 5 V. E. S.	
"	18th		Evacuated 2 Horses to No 5 V. E. S.	

No. 33 MOBILE VETERINARY SECTION No. ...... Date ......

D. D. & L., London, E.C. (A8001) Wt. W1771/M2031 750,000 5/17 Sch. 52 Forms/C2118/14

Instructions regarding War Diaries and Intelligence Summaries are contained in F. S. Regs., Part II. and the Staff Manual respectively. Title pages will be prepared in manuscript.

Sheet 2.

WAR DIARY
or
INTELLIGENCE SUMMARY.
(Erase heading not required.)

Army Form C. 2118.

33rd Mobile Vety Section

January 1919

Place	Date	Hour	Summary of Events and Information	Remarks and references to Appendices
DREUIL	19th		Routine Duties	
"	20th		Do Do.	
"	21st		Evacuated 3 Horses & 2 Hides to No. 5 V. E. S.	
"	22		Routine Duties	
"	23rd		Pte Grinham injured in motor car collision & taken to 65th Fld Ambce	
"			Paid men of Section.	
"	24th		Routine Duties	
"	25th		Do Do.	
"	26th		Do Do.	
"	27th		Pte Collings to be Major Macdonalds groom temporarily.	
"	28th		Routine Duties.	
"	29th		Evacuated 13 Horses & 5 Mules to 29th M.V.S.	
"	30th		Routine Duties	
"	31st		Do . Do	

No. 33 MOBILE ... VETERINARY SECTION No. ... Date ...

E S Pindar Capt. R.A.V.C.
O.C. 33rd Mobile Vety Section

D. D. & L., London, E.C.
(A8001) Wt. W1771/M2031 750,000 5/17 Sch. 52 Forms/C2118/14

14 21

9/8 33

C O N F I D E N T I A L.

WAR DIARY

OF

21 Div

33rd Mobile Veterinary Section, R.A.V.C.

FROM:- 1st February 1919, TO:- 28th February, 1919.

Army Form C. 2118.

Instructions regarding War Diaries and Intelligence Summaries are contained in F. S. Regs., Part II. and the Staff Manual respectively. Title pages will be prepared in manuscript.

WAR DIARY
or
INTELLIGENCE SUMMARY.
(Erase heading not required.)

33rd Mobile Vety Section

Sheet 1.

February 1919.

Place	Date	Hour	Summary of Events and Information	Remarks and references to Appendices
DREUIL	1st		Routine Duties	
LES-AMIENS.	2nd		Do Do.	
"	3rd		Do Do.	
"	4th		Evacuated 2 Horses to 29th M.V.S. Eleven Butcher animals handed to No 5 V.E.S.	
"	5th		Eight Butcher Animals handed to No 5 V.E.S. Pte W. Ginham No 28679 returned to Unit.	
"	6th		Two Butcher Do Do Do.	
"	7th		Six Do Do Do Do.	
"	8th		One Do Do Do Do.	
"	9th		Routine Duties	
"	10th		Do Do.	
"	11th		13 Horses & 4 Mules (Butchers) handed to No 5 V.E.S.	
"	12th		N.T.R.	
"	13th		1 Horse (Butcher) handed to No 5 V.E.S.	
"	14th		Pte Ginham W. No 28679 to Hospital	
"	15th		Three Mules & 2 Horses (Butchers) handed to No 5 V.E.S. One L.D. Horse to Animal Collecting Comp.	
"	16th		3 L.D. Horses to Animal Collecting Comp. One Mule to No 5 V.E.S.	
"	17th		Routine Duties.	
"	18th		4 Horses & 2 Mules to 5 V.E.S.	
"	19th		5 Horses to 29 M.V.S. also 8 Hides.	
"	20th		Routine Duties.	
"	21st		Driver A Stewart R.A.S.C. attached temporarily from No 1 Coy 21 Div Train. Private J Rees replaced Pte Collings A.S. as temporary groom to D.A.D.V.S.	
"	22nd		Left DREUIL at 9.30 A.M. arriving at HORNOY at 5 P.M.	

No. 33 MOBIL… VETERINARY SECTION

D. D. & L., London, E.C.
(A8001) Wt. W1771/M2031 750,000 5/17 Sch. 52 Forms/C2118/14

Instructions regarding War Diaries and Intelligence Summaries are contained in F. S. Regs., Part II. and the Staff Manual respectively. Title pages will be prepared in manuscript.

Sheet 2.

WAR DIARY 33rd Mobile Vety Section
or
INTELLIGENCE SUMMARY.
(*Erase heading not required.*)

February 1919.

Army Form C. 2118.

Place	Date	Hour	Summary of Events and Information	Remarks and references to Appendices
HORNOY	23rd		Routine Duties	
	24th		Do Do.	
	25th		Marking animals for sale.	
	26th		Routine Duties	
	27		Driver J W Coombes No 1 Coy 21 Div. Train replaced Driver A. Stewart R.A.S.C.	
	28th		Routine Duties.	

No. 33 MOBILE VETERINARY SECTION
No. ....
Date ....

E S Pindar, Captain R.A.V.C.
O.C. 33rd Mobile Vety Section.

D. D. & L., London, E.C.
(A8004) Wt. W1771/M2031 750,000 5/17 Sch. 52 Forms/C2118/14

28   21 Div.

WAR DIARY
or
INTELLIGENCE SUMMARY.
(Erase heading not required.)

Army Form C. 2118.

Instructions regarding War Diaries and Intelligence Summaries are contained in F. S. Regs., Part II. and the Staff Manual respectively. Title pages will be prepared in manuscript.

Sheet 1

33rd Mobile Vety Section
March 1919.

Vol 34

Place	Date	Hour	Summary of Events and Information	Remarks and references to Appendices
HORNOY	1st		Pte Keightley returned to 7th Leicester Batt.	
"	2nd		Pte A. S. Collings proceeded on leave in France.	
"	3rd		Routine Duties	
"	4th		Preparing animals for sale.	
"	5th		Sale of 100 animals at POIX.	
"	6th		Pte J. Rees returned to Section from D.A.D.V.S. Pte Debenham to D.A.D.V.S.	
"	7th		Preparing animals for sale at AUMALE.	
"	8th		Pte J Rees left section for Demobilization. Sale at AUMALE.	
"	9th		Routine Duties	
"	10th		Pte P Long proceeded on Special Leave.	
"	11th		Sale at POIX.	
"	12th		Routine Duties	
"	13th		Do Do	
"	14th		Pte W. Gunham returned to duty from Hospital.	
"	15th		Routine Duties	
"	16th		Pte A. S. Collings returned from leave.	
"	17th		Left HORNOY at 10 A.M. arriving at PICQUIGNY at 4 PM.	
PICQUIGNY	18th		Driver Coombes returned to Unit. Driver Gwynn attached from No 1 Coy 21 Div Train.	
"	19th		Evacuated 1 Sick Horse ~~from~~ to 29th M.V.S.	
"	20th		S/S Munn F. A. proceeded on leave in UK.	
"	21st		Routine Duties.	
"	22nd		Driver Gwynn S returned to No. 1 Coy ~~train~~. Evacuated 1 Sick Horse to 29 M.V.S.	
"	23rd		Demobilized 3 x Horses to Romdon Horse Camp.	
"	24th		Sergt Townsend left on Special leave to UK. Evacuated 1 Horse to No. 5 V.E.S	

No. 33 MOBILE VETERINARY SECTION No. ..... Date .....

Army Form C. 2118.

WAR DIARY
or
INTELLIGENCE SUMMARY.
(Erase heading not required.)

Instructions regarding War Diaries and Intelligence Summaries are contained in F. S. Regs., Part II. and the Staff Manual respectively. Title pages will be prepared in manuscript.

Sheet 2.

March 1919
33 Mob Vety Section

Place	Date	Hour	Summary of Events and Information	Remarks and references to Appendices
PICQUIGNY	25th		Routine Duties.	
"	26th		Evacuated 1 Mule to No. 54. E. S for Butcher.	
"	27th		Routine Duties	
"	28th		Evacuated 1 Sick Horse to 29 M. V. S.	
"	29th		Routine Duties.	
"	30th		Do Do.	
"	31st		Do Do.	

E. S. Rider Captain R.A.V.C.
O. C. 33 Mobile Vety Section.

No. 33 MOBILE VETERINARY SECTION
No. ....
Date ....

D. D. & L., London, E.C.
(A8001) Wt. W1771/M2031 750,000 5/17 Sch. 52 Forms/C2118/14

www.ingramcontent.com/pod-product-compliance
Lightning Source LLC
Chambersburg PA
CBHW081536160426
43191CB00011B/1774
9781474512107